BRITAIN AT WAR

UNSEEN ARCHIVES

BRITAIN AT WAR
UNSEEN ARCHIVES

MAUREEN HILL

PHOTOGRAPHS FROM THE

Daily Mail

This is a Parragon Book
First published in 2001

Parragon, Queen Street House, 4 Queen Street, Bath, BA1 1HE, UK

All photographs ©Associated Newspapers Ltd
Text ©Parragon

Produced by Atlantic Publishing
Designed by Judy Linard
Origination by Croxons PrePress

A catalogue record for this book is available from the British Library.
ISBN 0 75255 661 4
Printed in China

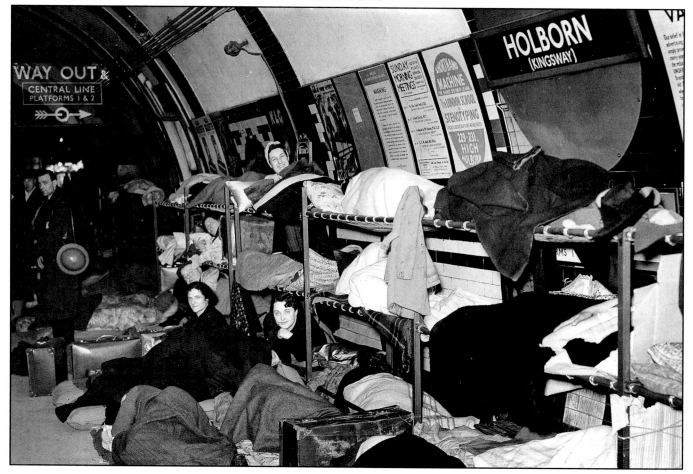

CONTENTS

INTRODUCTION
BRITAIN'S DARKEST AND FINEST HOUR

This book deals with many facets of Britain at war, building up a collage of images to give a comprehensive picture of what the country looked like, what the people experienced and how they responded to what was a time of great individual and national trauma.

The photographs, restored to original condition, are drawn from the vast archive of the Daily Mail. Some were taken to accompany the news stories of the day; some to accompany morale-boosting features; others are obvious propaganda. A few were published at the time; some never got past the censor and others had instructions in the censor's blue pencil about what had to be blanked or cropped out, and what details the accompanying captions could tell, or not tell. Individually, each photograph tells a story and many in sequence form a compelling narrative. In addition the scribbled notes and typed captions on the rear of each photograph tell many interesting, fascinating, funny and tragic tales to add to the visual images.

These notes and captions have often found their way into the captions in this book, wholly or in part. The way in which they are written gives a vivid idea of the viewpoint at the time and often gives a strong sense of immediacy to the photographs they accompanied. Where this material has been used it appears in quotation marks. Sometimes a date has been added in brackets to indicate what 'today' or 'yesterday' meant in the original caption.

Each of the nine chapters opens with an overview of the topic but the whole book gives a comprehensive insight into the war, its opening, progress and the landmarks towards a British and Allied victory. The book is essentially a collage of Britain at war, the 'Home Front', presenting a detailed view in words and pictures of what everyday life was like for those in Britain during the war.

Men's lives are portrayed principally in the 'In Uniform' chapter, as it was they who formed the bulk of the armed forces and the whole of the combat force. In 'Women in the Workforce' there is a focus on women's contribution to the war effort. And the experiences and contributions of children are detailed in 'A Wartime Childhood'. However, these chapters are not alone in cataloguing the lives and experiences of the population of Britain under the greatest threat to their way of life in a millennium.

The whole book, through its memorable photographs and its detailed text, evokes a picture of people's daily experience and amazing courage under pressure. It is a testament to the spirit and hardwork of the British people and the support they gained from their Allies in what was Britain's darkest and its finest hour.

ACKNOWLEDGEMENTS

The photographs in this book are from the archives of the *Daily Mail*.

That this book can be published is a tribute to the dedication of the staff, past and present, in the Picture Library at Associated Newspapers.

Particular thanks to Steve Torrington, Dave Sheppard, Brian Jackson, Alan Pinnock, Paul Rossiter and all the staff including:

John Bater	Rachel Swanston
Mark Ellins	David Lavington
David Stanley	Robert Sanders
Tom McElroy	Andrew Eva
Leslie Adler	Bill Beasley
Tony Fordham	Charles Whitbread
Steve Cooper	Philip Lambourne
Derek Drew	Katie Lee
Steve Murray	Chris Nelthorpe
Raymond Archer	Denise Hoy
Terry Aylward	Bob Dignum
Oscar Courtney	
Andrew Young	

Thanks also to
Christine Hoy, Judy Linard, Cliff Salter,
Richard Betts, Peter Wright, Trevor Bunting
Simon Taylor and Frances Hill.

BRITAIN AT WAR

UNSEEN ARCHIVES

Chapter One

THE OPENING MOVES

By the morning of the 3rd September 1939 war was inevitable. Prime Minister Neville Chamberlain broadcast to the nation at 11.15 a.m. that morning that 'this country is at war with Germany.' This declaration followed Britain's issuing of an ultimatum to Germany to withdraw from the Polish territory they had attacked and occupied in the early hours of the 1st September.

Less than a year earlier, at the end of September 1938, Neville Chamberlain had negotiated a peace deal in Munich with Adolf Hitler in which Britain conceded to the German annexation of Sudetenland. Keen to avoid a second war with Germany only twenty years since the end of the 'Great War', Chamberlain agreed that those parts of Czechoslovakia's Sudentenland occupied by ethnic Germans could become part of German territory. He returned from the talks in Munich to declare, 'I believe it to be peace in our time.'

The threat and outbreak of war brought immediate effects on most of the population. Fear of aerial bombardment, first seen in the First World War and developed by the Germans in the Spanish Civil War, provoked a mass evacuation of children, young mothers and pregnant women from the major cities. Whether one of the evacuated, one of those left behind in the cities, or one of those that housed the evacuees, this process meant huge emotional and practical upheaval.

By the second week in September troops of the British Expeditionary Force had crossed the Channel to meet up with French forces and moved to defend the Belgian border. These were regular and reserve soldiers, well trained but poorly equipped. Although throughout there had been some preparations for war, the years between the end of the Great War, the 'war to end all wars', and 1939 had seen a cutting down on defence spending, so that when war did come the military were not in a state of readiness.

After the initial flurry of activity in September there was little action in 1939. The term 'phoney war' was coined to reflect the fact that neither the Allies nor the Germans took any major initiatives. The British Expeditionary Force sat, alongside their allies, cold and bored in trenches in France. It was largely quiet in the air also; no bombing raids had materialised. Evacuees drifted back to their homes in the cities. Only at sea were there any sustained attacks by the Germans who used their U-boats and magnetic mines to threaten the British merchant fleet and challenge the Royal Navy.

While there was no official rationing until 8th January 1940, the consequences of the German campaign at sea had an early effect on consumers. Imported luxury items became scarce and eventually disappeared from the shelves. Home production of everything inessential ceased too as manufacturing changed to produce the weapons of war. Rationing started with butter, sugar and bacon, but extended to include many other basic foodstuffs, clothes and household items.

On the fighting front it was not until 9th April 1940 that Hitler made any moves. This time it was Denmark and Norway, swiftly followed by attacks on the Low Countries and then France. This blitzkrieg or 'lightning war' saw the defeat of Allied troops: 2000 German soldiers trained in winter warfare forcing the withdrawal of a 13,000 strong Allied force at Trondheim in Norway; and most famously, the evacuation of troops of the British Expeditionary Force and their allies from the beaches of Dunkirk between the 28th May and 3rd June. It took just ten days, from 10th to 20th May, for the Germans to occupy most of Holland, Belgium and Luxembourg, moving on into France. A week later British and French troops were pushed into a small pocket on the coast of France around Dunkirk. It was thought that Operation Dynamo, as the rescue mission was codenamed, could rescue fewer than 50,000 troops – in the event 338, 226 men were saved.

The blitzkrieg had profound political effects in Britain as well as in continental Europe. Chamberlain was a political casualty, resigning his Premiership when he had failed to prevent the German occupation of Norway, Denmark, Holland, Belgium and Luxembourg. On 10th May, Winston Churchill took over as Prime Minister at the head of a coalition government.

Back in Britain the troops rescued from the beaches were hailed as heroes, Churchill turning the defeat at Dunkirk into a victory of the British Spirit. Eight hundred civilian vessels had joined the 222 naval ships in Operation Dynamo. However, while the men had been rescued, their equipment was not and Britain faced the

People gather in the street outside the Houses of Parliament to hear news of Prime Minister Neville Chamberlain's speech to the Commons on the 2nd September. There was an expectation that, following the invasion of Poland on the previous day, the PM would announce an ultimatum to Germany to withdraw. The failure to do so was derided in the House of Commons and, following late night talks in cabinet, the demand was delivered to Berlin at 9.00 a.m. on the 3rd with a deadline for compliance set at 11.00 a.m. of the same day. When the regime in Germany failed to suspend the attack on Poland Britain declared war.

Outside the Royal Exchange the Town Clerk reads the Royal Proclamation calling on men up to the age of 36 to register for military service. The call-up started in June 1939 and was made possible by a Bill passed in May.

indeed the RAF not only helped save Britain from invasion but they also bought time for the army to re-group and begin to re-arm itself. On 1st January 1940 two million men between the ages of 20 and 27 had been conscripted or 'called up' and most of those were still undergoing training while the retreat from France was taking place. Conscription for military service extended throughout the war to include adult men up to the age of 50. In 1941 all 'mobile' women, that is women without carer responsibilities, between the ages of 20 and 30 were called up. Not all those conscripted were expected to go into the fighting forces, many were sent to do essential war work in factories or administration or even, like the 'Bevin Boys', in the coal mines.

Everyday life for the majority of the population changed, starting with everyday occupations. If not employed in an essential or 'reserved' occupation men found themselves conscripted into the forces, or their factory or trade pressed into serving the war effort. Women, who before the war had been a small part of the workforce, became the majority of the workforce, in

possibility of an invasion and blitzkrieg with an army lacking in weapons.

Operation Sea Lion was Hitler's codename for the invasion of Britain. The 15th of September was the date for the invasion by sea, the tides being most favourable on that date. In order for troop ships to land unharried by air attack, the Luftwaffe needed to destroy the RAF's capability. So began the 'Battle of Britain'. For much of the summer of 1940 the skies over southern England were witness to dogfights between British and German planes, but the air war took place over much of continental Europe. By the day set for the invasion the RAF had lost 915 planes, the Luftwaffe, 1733.

Churchill said of the skill and bravery of the pilots in the Battle of Britain 'never in the field of human conflict was so much owed by so many to so few'. And

Another call-up Proclamation being read outside the Mansion House. It is interesting to note the expressions on the faces in this photograph – the two civilian men in the background look considerably more worried than the women.

Crowds gather outside Downing Street on the morning of the
3rd September as the declaration of war is made.

the factories, on the land, in administrative jobs, service
industries. Even women at home, looking after
children, the sick or the elderly were expected to
contribute to the war effort by assembling small
machine parts at home. Children's schooling was
interrupted and they too had to contribute in a variety
of ways, such as helping with harvest or collecting
materials for recycling.

One year on, and by September 1940 the war had
affected everyone through absence or loss of loved
ones, changing patterns of life, shortages and rationing
of food, clothing, household items, and the constant
fear of invasion or aerial attack. This fear was finally
realised in August 1940 when bombing raids began on
British cities and towns. London was attacked on the
25th August; the RAF retaliated with a raid on Berlin.
Twenty-one British towns and cities were targeted by
the Luftwaffe on the 27th August. On 7th September
London suffered the first in a series of raids which
became known as the London Blitz. In November of
1940 the Germans widened their targets to include
cities and towns such as Coventry, Southampton,
Liverpool, Glasgow, Bristol and Birmingham. The Blitz
had arrived across Britain.

Opposite page: Evacuation began even before the declaration
of war and this group of children from the Hugh Myddelton
School in Clerkenwell were photographed on 1st September, the day
Hitler invaded Poland. The children all carry their gas masks
in cases and on many can be seen the luggage labels which helped
identify them.

WAR DECLARED

Opposite page top left: War was declared on Sunday, 3rd September and on Monday, 4th September there was a rush on the shipping companies as Americans, holidaying or living in Britain, sought to book a passage home. Here crowds gather outside the United States Line in Haymarket.

Opposite page top right: Quite quickly messages of support for the decision to declare war on Germany appeared. This one was photographed on 6th October 1939.

Opposite page below: On the same day that the Americans started leaving, the German Embassy in Carlton Terrace moved out.

Above: Police hold back the crowds in Downing Street on the morning of 3rd September.

Left: People rush for the nearest air raid shelter as the first air raid warning sounds, soon after the Prime Minister declared war.

SMILE AS YOU WAVE ME GOODBYE

Above: These smiling children are being evacuated in June 1940 during the Battle of Britain from a coastal town in the South-East.

Right: Blackout. The special screen fitted to street lamps to give a 'subdued moonlight'.

Opposite page top left: Mother and the baby of the family have to stay behind while sister joins her schoolmates on a train bound for Yorkshire.

Opposite page above right: A soldier comforts a child, perhaps his son, as these youngsters are evacuated from London.

Opposite page bottom: A poignant photograph on the emotional effects of evacuation, captioned: 'The pathetic scene at Waterloo Station this morning (1st September 1939) showing mothers shouting goodbye to their kiddies from behind the gates of the platform. No mothers were allowed on the platform as the kiddies embarked on the trains.'

REMEMBER YOUR GAS MASK

Left: Everyone had been issued during the months before the start of the war with a gas mask - a total of 38 million, with Mickey Mouse-faced ones for young children and complete suits for babies. It was an offence not to carry your gas mask at all times but many were forgotten, ending up as lost property, as this photograph of Baker Street Lost Property Office bears witness.

Above: Workmen sticking paper trellising onto a shop window to minimise damage from flying glass when the expected bombing came.

Top right: There never was an enemy attack of poison gas and masks were gradually dispensed with despite campaigns to try to persuade the population to carry them at all times. Richmond Council had to give notice of this 'surprise' practice attack.

Below right: Taken in the first few weeks of the war this photograph was captioned to put an emotional perspective on the war: 'Despite war-time conditions and difficulties in the life of the nation, human besides industrial life goes on. And in it women play a no lesser part than men.'

UNDER WRAPS FOR THE DURATION

Above: Part of the preparations in anticipation of aerial bombardment was that many of the great civic statues and landmarks had to be protected. Here work takes place on the statue of King Charles I just across from Trafalgar Square. The timber-framed construction, filled with sandbags and faced with corrugated iron cost £320 stated the First Commissioner of Works in answer to a question in the House of Commons in December 1939.

Right: The completed structure, protecting the equestrian statue of Charles I. Behind, in Trafalgar Square, the National Gallery, and the lions still sit boldly on their plinths.

Opposite page above: The boarded-up statue of Eros and the 'Dig for Victory' banner are the only signs of war in this picture of Piccadilly Circus.

Opposite page below: At work in October 1939 to protect the statue of Eros at Piccadilly Circus.

YOU'RE IN THE ARMY NOW

Above: 'The first batch of men aged 22 but not yet 23 reported at various military centres today (15th January 1940) for training.'

Left: 22nd June, 1940 and 30,000 more men registered for military service at Labour exchanges throughout the country.

Opposite page top left: Men born in 1911, aged 28 in June 1940 sign on. Here an Auxiliary Fire Service man signs on along with civilians.

Opposite page top right: August 1939 and 10 days before the outbreak of war, the call up notices are being prepared for those who will become liable for military service on 15th September.

Opposite page below: Sombre looking 36-year-old men sign on in January 1941.

DEFENDING THE HOME FRONT

Left: People gather on Tooting Bec Common to hear Charles Remnant calling for volunteers to join the 'Citizen's Army'.

Below: The Citizen's Army, an early initiative in a defence force to protect the Home Front, hold their first parade on Tooting Bec Common, dressed in civilian clothes and 'armed' with sticks and umbrellas.

Opposite page above: A Local Defence Volunteer parade just a month before the LDV were officially renamed, in July 1940, as the Home Guard. Many of those who joined up were veterans of the Great War as this parade testifies – the men proudly display their medals and march with the carriage of soldiers.

Opposite page below: Local Defence Volunteers march across a local parade ground in Balham. They are weaponless but some have LDV armbands and soldiers' caps.

ITALY DECLARES WAR

Opposite page top: When Italy declared war on Britain on 10th June 1940, there were anti-Italian demonstrations. These crowds gathered in front of an Italian café in Soho where windows had been smashed the night before.

Opposite page bottom left: The Italian community, many of whom had been settled in Britain for years, responded to the anti-Italian demonstrations by removing any symbols of nationality. This barber's shop in Soho is removing the shop sign with Italian language banner.

Opposite page bottom right: The same barber makes certain that no one thinks this is an Italian-owned shop.

Right: Treasures from the National Gallery were evacuated to a disused slate mine in North Wales.

Below: Vapour trails from over 100 enemy aircraft captured on camera while making a vain daylight attempt to reach London during the Battle of Britain.

DRAMA IN THE SKIES ABOVE DOVER

A barrage balloon shot down by German planes over Dover Castle.

Opposite top: 'A Nazi 'plane attempting to pierce defences in a London area was shot down and crashed on this house. The woman occupant was sheltering in the passage and escaped unhurt.'

Opposite bottom left: The damage to this school was incurred in June shortly after Churchill had told the nation that the Battle of Britain was about to begin.

Opposite bottom right: These houses in 'a town in the North Riding' of Yorkshire were damage by a raid at the end of May 1940.

ENEMY AIRCRAFT DOWNED OVER SUSSEX

A Luftwaffe plane shot down in August 1940 after an air battle with Spitfires over Sussex.

Above: Vapour trails from a Spitfire patrol. The planes patrolled night and day 'circling up high, ready to pounce on enemy raiders'.

Opposite top left: The plane crashed in flames. Auxiliary Fire Service men were summoned and put the fire out.

Opposite top right: During the Battle of Britain newspapers kept a running tally of the planes and airmen lost on both sides.

Opposite: This wreck of a Messerschmitt 110 fighter-bomber crashed at Bridgeham Farm near Horley in Surrey. It had been shot down in a raid on Croydon. The Censor allowed only the general area of 'South-East England' to be revealed.

NO. 13,85

175
(and more)
DOWN

MORE than 175 German 'planes and at least 350 airmen were shot down in the morning and afternoon attacks on London yesterday.

The R.A.F. lost 30 machines and 20 airmen.

In addition, German losses include:

18
on Saturday

Million

GR
Half R

350
175

HITLER'S
raids y
the most sha

The Air
between 350 a
were launched

SHOT DOWN IN A DOG-FIGHT

Left: Bullet holes from a Spitfire's machine guns on the Nazi swastika can be clearly seen on the wreckage of this plane.

Below: This Luftwaffe fighter plane is guarded closely by soldiers. Its relatively good condition would be able to reveal information about enemy aircraft.

Opposite top: This German mine-laying plane crashed at Clacton and exploded, destroying many houses.

Opposite middle left: 'The pilot of this Messerschmitt 109 fighter claimed three victories. Each of the white bars on the tail denotes one. The pilot was out to get his fourth on Saturday, but he met his match over south-east England. His squadron's crest carried the motto "Gott Strafe England."'

Opposite middle right: Brought down by anti-aircraft fire this plane broke up and wreckage was strewn across a railway line in South-East England.

Opposite bottom: A Messerschmitt 109 shot down in raids over Ramsgate draws civilians and the military.

MESSERSCHMITT REACHES PARLIAMENT

Below: 'Not how the pilot of this Messerschmitt would have liked to have seen Westminster. A German machine being taken through London on its way to the scrap heap today.'

Opposite above: The farmer carries on his work of rounding up the sheep around the wreckage of a German plane which had been shot down after a dog-fight over the farm. Local Defence Volunteers and soldiers were on the scene immediately and took the pilot away.

Opposite below: A Junkers 88 lies in a cornfield after being brought down by a Polish airman near the North-East Coast. Its crew, some of whom were injured, were taken prisoner.

Right: The man on the ladder is searching a tree for bits of the Junkers 88.

RECONNAISSANCE PLANE SHOT DOWN NEAR DALKEITH

Above: This German plane on a reconnaissance flight was brought down by British fighter planes near Dalkeith in Scotland. The pilot survived unhurt, but two of the crew died.

Right: An RAF corporal inspects the bullet holes in the tail of the plane shot down near Dalkeith.

Opposite top: This German plane crashed near the coast of North-East England.

Opposite bottom: An Messerschmitt 109 shot down by British fighter planes after it had crossed the South-East coast.

Chapter Two

THE BLITZ

One of the most enduring images of Britain at war is that of bombed cities and towns, the destruction and devastation caused by aerial bombardment, whether from Luftwaffe planes or from the rocket bombs developed late in the war by Germany. The real Blitz covered a nine month period from September 1940 until May 1941, during which 43,000 British civilians lost their lives. By June 1941 German planes were needed to fight elsewhere with the opening of a second front as Germany attacked its former ally, the Soviet Union.

Later raids in 1942, the so-called Baedeker raids came in retaliation for the saturation bombing of German cities such as Cologne. The final threat from the skies came with the development of the V-rockets. These unmanned rockets, nicknamed 'doodlebugs' or 'buzz bombs', could be fired during daylight hours from bases in France, reaching a large area of southern England. The D-Day landings and the liberation of France put paid to the V-rocket menace.

The Blitz began in earnest on the 7th September 1940 with the first in a series of attacks on London which lasted for fifty-six days. Initially the raids took place during the day and night but German losses were large and after a week the bulk of the bombing took place under cover of darkness. The raids up to the 15th September were part of the strategy to defeat and destroy the RAF in order to clear the skies of British planes to protect German troop ships in an invasion from the sea.

After the 15th September the other platforms in the Germans' strategies became important. As the home of the British Government it was intended that bombing the capital would damage the administrative heart and thus the conduct of the war. However, the symbolic importance of damage to London, the centre of Britain, the Commonwealth and the Empire could not be overestimated. Much of the bombing was centred on the Port of London, damaging shipping and causing many civilian casualties. Part of the intended results by the High Commands on both sides was that the death and destruction caused by bombing would severely damage morale and that the populations would urge their governments to sue for peace.

Casualties in London, while high, 13,000 killed and 20,000 injured in September and October alone, were reduced by the availability of deep shelters in the London Underground system. Tube stations became the preferred shelters, although initially the government were averse to the system being used for this purpose, believing it would seriously compromise the Underground's ability to function. Government were also anxious that a 'deep shelter mentality' did not develop. However, public demand and the clear evidence that the city and its people could still function, changed their minds.

Life for most Londoners during the closing months of 1940 became a relentless routine of going into shelters almost as soon as dusk fell, sleeping or dozing through the night, listening to the raids outside and emerging in

Operations board from the War Cabinet HQ under Storey's Gate, bearing the date that marked the beginning of the Battle of Britain. It was to here that Churchill and his Ministers would retire when there was a raid, protected 40 ft below ground by 17ft-thick concrete walls reinforced with old rails.

the morning to see the extent of the damage. Days were spent at work, or clearing up the remains of bombed homes and workplaces, or trying to look after a family at home or, for those made homeless, in temporary accommodation in public buildings such as schools and church halls.

One of the most devastating raids on London took place right at the end of the year. It was a Sunday night and the Thames was at its lowest ebb tide. High explosive parachute mines severed the water mains at the beginning of the raid, during which more than 10,000 firebombs were dropped on the City of London. The result was the second Fire of London. One of the most powerful images of the war was captured that night – the image of St Paul's standing untouched amid the flames and smoke. It was taken from the roof of the Daily Mail building by photographer Herbert Mason.

London suffered many more nights of bombing over the next few months until May 1941. On the night of May 11th over 500 Luftwaffe planes dropped hundreds of high explosive bombs and tens of thousands of incendiary devices. Many important London landmarks were damaged that night, including the chamber of the House of Commons and Big Ben. This was the last great bombing raid on London, although the fear of the attackers returning remained for many years.

The last raid on London was the culmination of a Spring bombing offensive which saw many British cities and towns targeted. The provinces had not been spared bombing and some, like the ancient cathedral city of Coventry, suffered nights of bombing just as intense as that on the capital. After a raid on 14th November 1940 Coventry's cathedral was almost entirely reduced to rubble, along with many other buildings in the city centre. The Luftwaffe had dropped 600 tons of high explosives and thousands of incendiaries from a squad of around 400 bombers.

The Coventry bombing was part of a change in tactic by German High Command. As well as raiding the symbolic heart of the nation, the industrial base of the country was targeted in an attempt to destroy the means by which Britain could continue to prosecute the war. Birmingham, Sheffield, Manchester, Glasgow and other centres of aircraft, military vehicle, weapon and munitions production suffered devastating raids. So too did the ports like Southampton, Bristol and Liverpool as the naval dockyards and navy and merchant ships were targeted.

Demoralising the British public was a major aim in all the bombing and it was indeed a frightening experience for many. Bombing affected everyone's life. Loss of life, loss of homes, loss of workplaces, loss of important civic landmarks, loss of sleep, loss of peace of mind, for you could never be sure when the bombers might strike and what it was you might lose. Nevertheless, while the population lived with that fear, it did not become demoralised. In fact, it almost contributed to the reverse effect – the sense of a nation pulling together, for bombs did not discriminate, no one, not even the King and Queen in Buckingham Palace, was spared the effects or the fear.

The wreckage of a tram car damaged in a daylight raid in Blackfriars Road.

DAYLIGHT RAIDERS

Above: The anti-aircraft guns' fire power, supported by a Spitfire, brought down this Dornier close to a London station during a daylight raid on 16th September 1940. RAF officers inspect the wreckage of an engine and propeller - the tail unit broke off and fell over rooftops.

Left: This fighter-bomber was brought down almost intact, drawing onlookers in this London street.

BEATING THE BOMBERS

Above: An anti-aircraft battery at work in London during a raid.

Left: 'Piccadilly Circus. Hardly a pedestrian to be seen. Delayed action bombs in the vicinity caused this area to be closed to traffic.'

Opposite above: A raid on 18th September 1940 caused damage in Oxford Street. Firemen play their hoses on the National Bank.

Opposite below: The same raid also hit John Lewis's department store.

HEARTH AND HOME

Opposite page: The side of this house is blown away but the interior wall is almost untouched. The kitchen range on the first floor is topped by a clock and horse statues on the mantel. And upstairs the mirror on the wall is uncracked.

Above: An Eton boy moving his belongings after stray bombs dropped on the school in December 1940.

Top right: The Ring Sports Stadium at Blackfriars, damaged, along with houses in the neighbourhood, when two bombs fell on it during raids in October 1940. Remarkably no one was injured.

Middle right: Grose's sports shop in New Bridge Street in December 1940 produced this eerie wreckage where the blast had blown bicycles upwards, to hang from the rafters.

Bottom right: A valuable painting is rescued from the debris of a wrecked building.

BOMBERS HIT THE HOUSES OF PARLIAMENT

Left: Wreckage in Cloister Court caused by bombs which hit the Houses of Parliament during a twelve-hour raid on the capital by 413 aircraft in December 1940. The building to the left of the guard is the Member's Cloakroom.

Below: Damage to vehicles was not the only problem for the Transport authorities - damage to the infra-structure such as railway lines, tramlines and roadways was frequent. Here a railway bridge is wrecked.

Right: Public transport was also badly affected by the bombing. This bus was wrecked by falling masonry during a raid.

SALVAGING FROM THE WRECKAGE

Opposite page top left: Again in raids in October 1940, Whiteley's department store in Bayswater suffered severe damage - this shot shows part of the ground floor.

Opposite page top right: Home. A home in the London area demolished during a enemy night raid.

Opposite page below: Survivors are given a much needed cup of tea by a Salvation Army worker as they collect together their belongings from the wreckage of their home.

Left: A Mrs Mann lay asleep in bed when a bomb dropped on the rear of her cottage in outer London. She escaped uninjured.

Below: 'Mrs M. Robertson and her family removing articles from their wrecked house.'

BIGGEST BOMB CRATER AT BANK

Opposite page: The largest bomb crater in London. Troops crossing a temporary road bridge over the crater at Bank Tube station caused by a direct hit on the station on the night of 11th January 1941. At least fifty people were killed. The censor gave permission for this picture to appear in the newspapers on condition that all of the crater was blacked out, and only the road bridge, with the troops crossing it, was shown.

Above: Auxiliary Fire Service (AFS) men taking water from the Thames after a night raid in which many incendiaries were dropped.

Left: Debris in the road, including fallen masonry, but mostly dislodged cobblestones.

Below left: Londoners in the East End queue patiently to enter air raid shelters.

PIONEER CORPS

Above: Members of the Pioneer Corps refreshing themselves with tea and buns provided by the Salvation Army. Many of the Pioneers were recruited from the ranks of the unemployed and their task was to help the salvage and clearance operations after the raids.

Left: An unsafe office block being demolished to protect the public from the danger of falling masonry.

Opposite page above: March 1942. Despite two and a half years of war the public still supported the government, even pressing them in this demonstration to take a more active stance against the Nazis and open a second front.

Opposite page below: London carries on. Despite the bombing, the Union Jack still flies.

IN THE SHADOW OF THE TOWER

Left: One of the most devastating raids on London occurred on 29th December 1940. More than 10,000 fire bombs were dropped on the city on a night when the Thames was at its lowest and enemy aircraft had earlier in the evening hit the water mains. The 20,000 firemen fighting the blaze had to be reinforced by soldiers and civilians. Here the Pioneer Corps are clearing up around Tower Hill after the raid – the Tower of London can be seen in the background.

Above: St Anne's Parochial School, Hatton Garden ablaze as fire-fighters struggle to bring the flames under control.

Right: Aldermanbury, near the Guildhall, was a busy city street, home to the Wren church of St Mary the Virgin. That church, like the rest of the street, was devastated.

CITY DEVASTATED BY THE SECOND FIRE OF LONDON

Opposite page above: On New Year's Day 1941, the Lord Mayor of London inspects the damage in Aldermanbury.

Opposite page below: The Lord Mayor reaches the Guildhall on his tour inspecting the damage in the City.

Left: The Guildhall after the Fire of London. The medieval walls remained but the wooden roof, which was not as old as the walls, was lost.

Below: Debris inside the Guildhall Banqueting Hall. It was to take years of careful restoration work post-war to return the building to its former glory.

St. Clement Danes Church

NOTICE

This Church is dangerous, pending repairs, on account of falling pieces of brick and stone. The public are warned to keep away from the walls—those who enter, do so at their own risk, and must keep within the roped enclosure.

MORNING PRAYER & SERMON are held on Sunday Mornings at 11 a.m. in The Parish House, Portugal Street, near by.

History of the Church—Postcards etc., can be obtained from the Verger, 8, Clements Inn Passage.

THE SECRETARY OF THE PAROCHIAL CHURCH COUNCIL.

GUILDHALL LIBRARY SALVAGED

Opposite page: Books rescued from the 25,000-volume Guildhall Library, much of which was lost. However, the building itself survived to a remarkable extent. The worst damage was sustained by the roof which was much newer in origin than the historic walls, many of which remained intact.

Above left: St Bride's Church suffered damage during the raid.

Above right: Evidence that London carried on whatever the bombers might throw at it.

Left: Debris in the street and the smoking ruins on the morning of the 30th December.

CLEARING UP

Left: Royal Engineers clearing up by blowing up unsafe masonry on 3rd January 1941.

Below: A week after the raid the Duke of Kent (front, middle), later killed while serving as a pilot in the RAF, inspects the damage.

Opposite page top left: Even after the raid the public were not safe from explosions. Here the photographer has captured the moment a delayed action bomb went off on the outskirts of London. The houses had been damaged earlier and the street had been cordoned off.

Opposite page top right: Pictures from the dome. A series of pictures were taken from the dome of St Paul's Cathral on 3rd January 1941, surveying the damage from the raid.

Opposite page below: The City a year on from the Great Fire.

ST PAUL'S AMID THE RUINS

Opposite page: This picture looking towards St Paul's was taken a week after the Fire of London and the ruins are still smouldering.

Left: The City from the west of the Old Bailey - Justice with her scales is just visible.

Below: Although St Paul's escaped damage during the Great Fire, it was hit by German bombs during the course of the war. This crater in the north transept was made by a bomb dropped during a raid in April 1941.

NEW PERSPECTIVES

Left: A new perspective of St Paul's revealed when demolition crews dynamited dangerous buildings in Newgate Street.

Below: Just over a year on and the area around the cathedral is still being cleared. The salvaged bricks from Ludgate Hill and Pilgrim Street were used to build water dams.

Opposite page top: A new view of St Paul's revealed as the buildings in Ludgate Hill which used to obscure it were damaged or demolished.

Opposite page bottom: The thoroughfare in the centre of this picture of the area to the west of St Paul's is closed and used as a storage area for materials used in the making safe and rebuilding of the area.

NOBODY AT HOME

'A postman tries to deliver letters in historic Watling Street, Roman highway, in the city of London, after the latest indiscriminate Nazi raid.'

Opposite page top: The Blitzed area around St Paul's pictured in May 1943.

Opposite page bottom: Out of house and home. A family made homeless by the bombing sit in the street awaiting a removal van.

MOVING OUT

Below: Families sit in the street with all they have managed to save from their homes.

Left: 'Debris piled in the street, shattered window frames, and snake-like coil of firemen's hose, the scene in Fetter Lane, after one of the heaviest Nazi raids on the London area yet experienced.' This picture was taken on 12th May 1941 after what was, in effect, the last raid on London in the Blitz.

Opposite page top: Londoners salvage their belongings and chat in the street while a nun offers comfort.

Opposite page bottom: Moving out of a bombed-out home in Hendon.

BACK FROM BERLIN
- TO THIS

Below left: 'An RAF pilot, veteran of many flights over Germany, returned home to find it destroyed. With him are his father and sister who were slightly injured.'

Left: Miss Olive Unwin escaped unhurt from a raid which destroyed her Cambridgeshire home and ruined her trousseau.

Below right: Although their doorway was wrecked, this family escaped uninjured when bombs fell under 200 yards from their cottage in the Ashdown Forest.

Opposite page above: Residents of the Guinness Trust Buildings in the Kings Road, Chelsea, salvage their belongings.

Opposite page below: 'Still smiling. Londoners, who are evacuating themselves, together with their belonging, enjoy a read on the tailboard of a removal van.'

HOMELESS IN SOUTHAMPTON

Left: Dealing with the homeless after raids on Southampton.

Above left: This family, who were bombed out of their Westminster home in April 1941, were billeted in a '£100-a-week Park-Lane luxury flat.'

Above right: This door fell on a Miss Muddle as she ran from her home when an enemy plane crashed.

Opposite page top: Office workers enjoying a basin of soup provided by the American Food Convoys. This picture was taken in May 1941 and the USA had not entered the war but was supporting Britain in other ways such as the Lend-Lease Agreement signed in March 1941.

Opposite page below: Homeless children queuing for a free hot bath. This service, including free soap and towels, was provided by Lever Brothers.

BOMBS ON BUCKINGHAM PALACE

Left: It was not only ordinary people who were affected by the bombing. The King and Queen remained in residence throughout the war and the Palace was hit by bombs several times. In September 1940 this crater outside the gates was caused by one of five bombs dropped in the vicinity.

Below: The North Lodge, next to Constitution Hill, received a direct hit in a raid in March 1941. A policeman died when one of the stone pillars fell on him.

Opposite page: A policeman shows off damage caused by a bomb dropping on the Palace's North Lodge which can be seen behind the railings.

EMERGENCY WASHING SERVICE

Top left: Free clothes-washing service for those made homeless by the bombing.

Middle left: Waiting patiently for instructions after their workplace was destroyed in a raid beneath posters promoting War Savings. By March 1942 Britain had spent £9050 million on the war - ordinary people's savings as well as their taxes had helped to pay the costs.

Top right: A lucky escape! A live pet rabbit discovered in the bomb debris after a raid in Cambridgeshire.

Left: Villagers in East Anglia gather round a crater made by a bomb that killed a pony and a cow.

Opposite page top: A delayed action bomb startled these women.

Opposite page below: Clacton Pier damaged by a bomb.

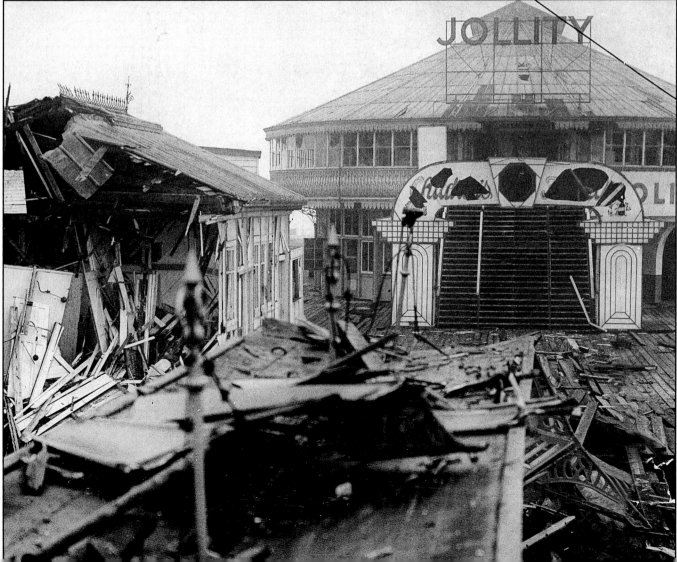

VICTIMS

Top left: A child victim of the bombing is cared for by a nurse at Queen Mary's Hospital, Sidcup. She was in a group of school children hit during a daylight raid on their school, Sandhurst Road School in Catford. Thirty-eight children were killed.

Top far left: Houses damaged in Clacton by a mine-laying plane which crashed and the mines onboard blew up.

Middle far left: Mr and Mrs Calvert rest on a bench after being made homeless from their eight-roomed house which was destoyed in the Clacton disaster.

Bottom far left: These toddlers are the victims of 'bomb shock' and are being cared for at a convalescent home in Hertfordshire.

Left: An injured man is led away from danger.

Above: Examining one of the live mines from the plane which did not explode on impact in Clacton.

Right: The scene at the Sandhurst Road School in Catford as rescue workers strive to reach children and teachers.

HOSPITALS ARE BOMBING TARGETS

Left: A Mr E. Smith from the National Physical Laboratory searches the debris of this London hospital with an 'electric detector' for radium from damaged X-ray equipment.

Below: Salvaging whatever can be saved from the wards. Everything that could be saved and re-used was rescued, cleaned, mended or sent for recycling.

Opposite page top: Unfortunately, several casualties occurred when this hospital was bombed in November 1940.

Opposite page below: A wrecked ward in the London Chest Hospital.

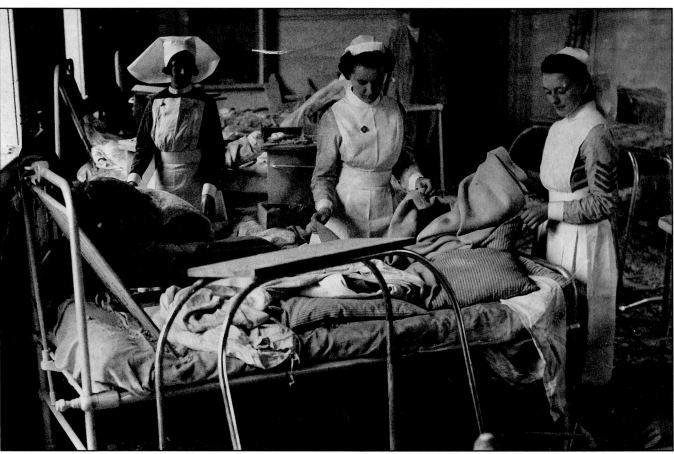

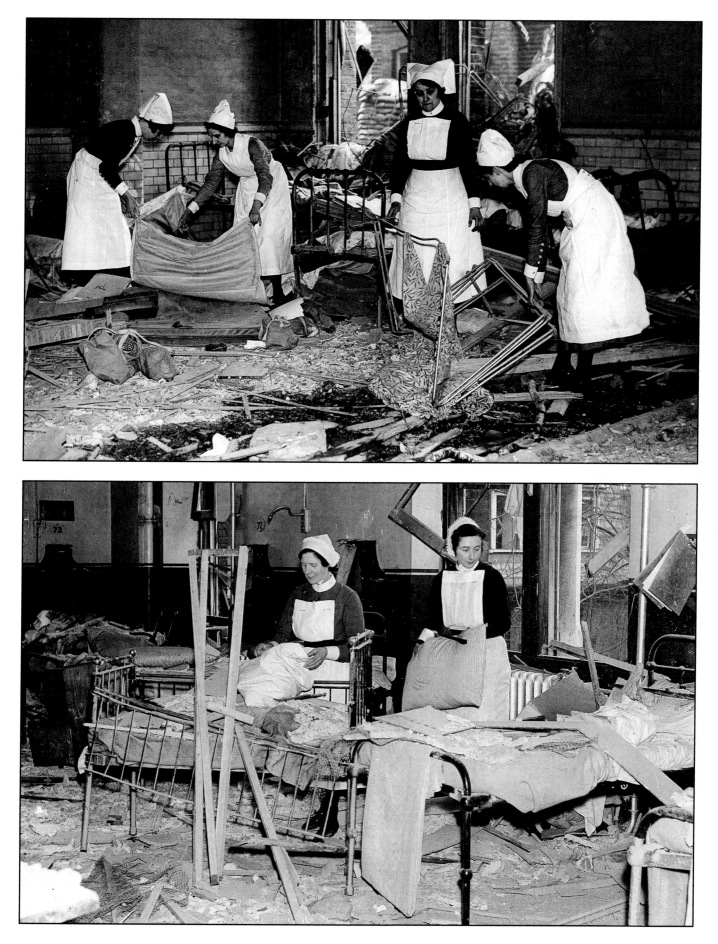

SALVAGING IN THE WARDS

Opposite page top: Four hospital wards were wrecked in this South-East London hospital in an early raid in the Blitz. Miraculously, no one was injured.

Opposite page bottom left: Remembrance Day 1940 - ATS planting poppies in memory of civilians killed during the war.

Opposite page bottom right and left: Nurses inspecting the damage at one of six hospitals hit during a raid in March 1941.

Below left: 8th April 1941. 'As usual a Hospital was one of the targets in last night's raid. Nurses salvaging in the debris of a London hospital for the aged and infirm.'

Below right: This notice was posted outside St Stephen's Hospital, Fulham. Three male wards were destroyed and several men were killed, but all the women were saved. Patients were rescued by nurses, who had been attending a dance, dressed in evening wear, working by torchlight.

BURYING THE DEAD IN COVENTRY

Top left: A hundred and seventy-two victims from the November 1941 Coventry raid were buried in a communal grave.

Top right: 'The twenty-six victims of the bombed village school were buried in a communal grave in Sussex today.' (Saturday, 3rd October 1942).

Left: The wreckage and the rubble left behind after a house has been hit by a bomb. The workmen's first job is salvaging materials for re-use and then carrying out repairs.

Opposite page: 'Stout wellingtons, tin hat and firm jaw - this lad sums up the resolve of a group of Londoners talking over last night's raid.'

BLITZ ON MANCHESTER

Opposite page top left and right: Fire fighters tackle a blaze during a raid on Manchester.

Opposite page far left: Northcliffe house, the Manchester offices of the Daily Mail, suffered damage in a raid in June 1941.

Opposite page left: Close up of the entrance to Northcliffe House on Deansgate.

Above: Wrecked buildings in Bosley Street, Manchester.

Right: Gunners from Cheshire's Inland Royal Artillery Unit rush to their gun at the sound of the alert.

SHEFFIELD HIT

Opposite page top: Sheffield United's Bramall Lane stand in January 1941, following raids in December 1940.

Opposite page bottom: The Sheffield Blitz on 12th December 1940 left virtually every tram car in the city with some degree of damage - 31 were totally destroyed.

Above: Damage in the centre of Manchester after the raids.

Left: Old Trafford wrecked by bombs.

LIVERPOOL'S CHRISTMAS BLITZ

Above: Liverpool and the Birkenhead area suffered two nights of heavy attack on 20th and 21st December 1940. Over two hundred people were killed in these raids.

Right: A bomb crater in the back yard of a house in the North Riding of Yorkshire.

Opposite page top: Troops assisting with clearing up the damage after the December 12th raid. In what was a frequent pattern in the Germans' bombing strategy, the raiders returned to Sheffield on 15th December after a brief respite, just enough time to begin the clear-up operation.

Opposite page bottom: Debris left in Liverpool after the demolition squad had made the area safe.

BAEDEKER RAIDS

Opposite page top left: The 15th-century Guildhall in York burning fiercely after a raid in a series in retribution for RAF attacks on Baltic ports. These raids took place in April and May of 1942 and targets seemed to have been selected for their historic interest from the Baedeker Tourist Guide Book. Exeter, Bath and Norwich, were targeted alongside York.

Opposite page top right: A church in York after a Baedeker Raid. Damage was severe in these provincial towns and cities as they had fewer air defences than other more likely targets.

Opposite page left: Stray bombs fell behind these houses in a North Riding town, demolishing outhouses and bringing slates off the roofs.

Above: Damage to Middlesbrough Railway Station after a bombing raid in November 1942.

Right: An air raid in Hull in July 1941 caused extensive damage in New Bridge Road, a residential district.

THE RUINS OF COVENTRY CATHEDRAL

Opposite page: Coventry Cathedral in November 1940 after the devastating raid on the fourteenth.

Left: The burned-out interior of St Nicholas Church, Liverpool which was hit by a number of incendiary bombs in a raid on 20th December.

Below: A café and shops were wrecked when a bomb dropped on this unidentified North-East coastal town. People in the buildings were brought out when rescue workers dug a hole into the basement.

RAIDS ON THE MIDLANDS

Top left: Coventry's citizens go about their business through the ruins of their city streets less than 48 hours after the raid.

Middle left: YMCA vans serving tea to the people of Coventry amid the wreckage of their city.

Bottom left: This was a shopping street in Coventry.

Above: Salvaging the contents of a home wrecked in the 11-hour raid on Birmingham on the night of 22nd November 1940. Birmingham, as a major manufacturing centre, was an obvious target. Transport and telephone systems were badly affected but it was damage to the water system which caused the most urgent problem - firefighters had to rely on pumping water from the canals or leave some fires to burn themselves out.

Opposite page: Firemen still at work on a Birmingham factory the morning after the raid.

COVENTRY'S SHOPPING CENTRE

Opposite page above: One of Coventry's main shopping areas still smouldering on the morning after the Blitz. In an attack that lasted 13 hours 600 tons of high explosives and thousands of incendiaries were dropped by a squad of around 400 Luftwaffe bombers.

Opposite page below: Damage to a shopping arcade in Birmingham.

Above: The interior of a shelled church in Dover.

Left: Mr and Mrs Dykes inspecting the damage to their home after an air battle on the South-East coast during the Battle of Britain.

CAMBRIDGESHIRE

Top left: Eight houses were destroyed in this raid in Cambridgeshire, and nine people lost their lives.

Above and middle left: Sifting through the wreckage after the raid. It was important not only to salvage survivors' belongings but also to reclaim building materials.

Bottom left: The occupant of this bed, a Mrs Chapman, aged 74, of the Home Counties, escaped injury when she got out of bed and went to the shelter. She had just made it to the shelter when the bomb dropped.

Opposite page top: This Dornier which had machine-gunned streets in a coastal town was brought down on a beach. This area of South-East England was known as 'Hell Corner', coming under daily attacks in the weeks before the change of tactics and the shift to raids on major cities.

Opposite page bottom left: Homes in Dover damaged by shells from German long-range guns.

Opposite page bottom right: Elegant homes close to the Dover seafront damaged and abandoned.

DOVER AT MERCY OF GERMAN LONG-RANGE GUNS

Top: 'The coast of S. E. England as seen by the Germans across the Channel.'

Middle left: As soon as France fell Dover could be reached by German guns on the other side of the Channel as well as by Luftwaffe bombers. Here a shell explodes in a Dover street.

Middle right: This home in Southern England was damaged in the first wave of flying bombs, nicknamed 'doodlebugs' or 'buzz bombs', in June 1944, exactly a week after the D-Day landings.

Bottom left: A Dover sea-front hotel damaged by shelling. The censor did not pass this picture for publication.

Opposite page: This captured German airman, part of a large group passing through London stations in October 1940, hides his face from the cameras.

LUFTWAFFE AIRMEN CAPTURED

Opposite page: These Luftwaffe airmen were being escorted through a London station during October 1940. At this stage the claim was made by Lord Croft that 'more German airmen have been slain or captured than civilians'.

Above: This picture of two iron-crossed German airmen is ironically captioned: 'More Luftwaffe visitors here.'

Right: A German airman, shot down over South-East England is escorted to the railway station before embarking on his journey to a POW camp.

Chapter Three

PROTECTING THE HOME FRONT

From early in 1939 plans for Civil Defence in the event of war were beginning to develop. Air raid shelters were delivered to thousands of homes and plans were made to evacuate children and some women from areas thought to be at risk of bombing. Twelve regional Civil Defence commissioners were also appointed with special powers to govern their areas if they should become cut off from central government.

Many of the early Civil Defence measures were related to the threat of aerial bombardment. There was a real fear that Luftwaffe planes would drop explosive, incendiary and poison gas bombs. In the months preceding the outbreak of war 38 million gas masks were distributed. There were Mickey Mouse-faced ones for young children and complete respirator suits for babies. It was an offence not to carry a gas mask at all times but as the war wore on and a gas attack never came the only times the public ever wore them were in practice drills and mock attacks. Soon they were forgotten items.

In opinion polls the one thing consistently cited as most inconvenient about the war was another Civil Defence priority - the Blackout. It was necessary in order to make it as difficult as possible for enemy aircraft to sight their targets. Windows had to be covered so that no chink of light escaped. Vehicle lights had to be dimmed and only project downwards. Streetlamps were fitted with a special screen which dimmed their light. These lamps and the painting of kerb edges white did not prevent a number of deaths caused by people walking into solid objects in the dark.

Patrolling the Blackout was one of the major tasks of Air Raid Protection (ARP) wardens. Each warden would be responsible for a small area, perhaps only a few streets. The wardens had to deal with the immediate aftermath of a bomb falling on their patch, informing central control, organising ambulances, fire and rescue services. They would also be expected to administer first aid and to ensure that people remained calm at any incident.

ARP wardens were also responsible for the public shelters in their area. Many people had shelters in their own home or garden. The classic Anderson shelter, only four square metres in size, was planted in the garden and covered with half a metre of soil. Other shelters, like the Morrison shelter, were constructed within the house but often people sheltered in cellars, basements and stairwells. Large public shelters sometimes had heating, lighting, toilets and a few had canteens. Sleep was always a problem - private shelters were stuffy and lacking in basic facilities, public shelters were noisy and full of restless people. The tunnels of the London Underground became a popular shelter for many Londoners during the Blitz, despite initial government attempts to discourage their use.

While most people were safe in shelters during an air raid or asleep in their beds on quiet nights there were large numbers of people on duty every night. ARP wardens were supported by other workers and volunteers such as the fire services. On many nights the dedication of the fire services saved many lives

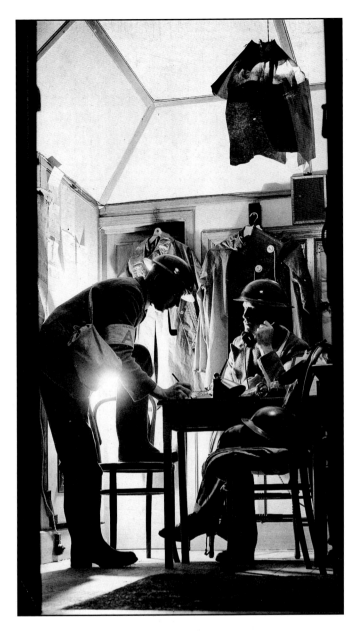

'Keepers of the night. An ARP outpost in Essex. These men start their duty at midnight and are seen in their hut taking messages.' Note the Blackout shade on the light.

and a great deal of property. Incendiary bombs caused the most work for fire crews but explosive bombs could also cause fires, especially if they ruptured a gas main.

Teams of roof spotters were on duty nightly to watch for enemy aircraft as the quickest way of keeping factories and institutions informed of the likelihood of an attack. Those involved in such duties had to take part in aircraft recognition training. Those in the Observer Corps were also trained in spotting enemy aircraft, as well as looking for signs of an enemy

invasion. The Corps was closely affiliated with the military and acted as extra eyes and ears, relaying information to Fighter Command.

One of the most enduring images of the Civil Defence strategy is that of the Home Guard, or Dad's Army as it was affectionately known. In May 1940 as the Blitzkrieg in Europe took place and the British Expeditionary Force was pushed back to the beaches at Dunkirk, the first formal Civil Defence force was set up. Originally called Local Defence Volunteers (LDV), by July 1940 Churchill had changed the name to the Home Guard. In the first few months after they were formed there were no uniforms, only armbands; no modern weapons, only old shotguns, pitchforks and sticks; and many of the volunteers were old men. However, many of those old men had combat experience, having served in the First World War. By the time it was disbanded in November 1944 the Home Guard was almost indistinguishable in its professionalism from the regular army - in uniform, well drilled, well armed and capable of taking on many of the duties the regular army had undertaken, such as defending sensitive installations and buildings.

The Home Guard's principal role was to defend the country from a threatened invasion. There were other threats to the country by people working to undermine the war effort from inside the country. One of the Police Force's many tasks was to keep a look-out for those promoting the Nazi way of life or spying for the Germans. The police had innumerable other roles, such as escorting prisoners of war. And while burglary and other peacetime crimes were much reduced there were other crimes such as blackmarket dealing that they had to investigate. Police were also very important in ensuring people remained calm in the aftermath of an air raid.

Air raids were the biggest threat to the public and it was in these areas that the greatest Civil Defence efforts were required. Any one incident could involve many people - ARP wardens, police, firefighters, rescue workers, doctors, nurses, ambulance staff. Once the raid had taken place and the people

A task for the police - signalling the 'All Clear'.

affected attended to both physically and emotionally there was a need for further work to make the environment safe for others. Demolition crews and those working to move rubble and debris often had a dangerous job. Royal Engineers were usually in charge of setting the controlled explosives which would bring down unsafe masonry but often unsafe walls were pulled down by hand.

KEEPING THE INVADER OUT

Opposite page: 'You are looking at the famous clock tower and the Houses of Parliament through a nearby barbed-wire entanglement - a symbolic picture that speaks of Britain's preparedness to withstand to the last any attempts at invasion.'

Right: A village post office has its name painted out as part of a 'nationwide scheme to present an anonymous Britain to any possible parachute invaders'.

Below: The name of a local railway station being painted out in June 1940, shortly after the retreat from Dunkirk when invasion was a real possibility.

SANDBAGGED!

Below: Taken on the day war was declared this shows residents filling sandbags to protect their homes in the expectation of early bombing raids.

Left: Possible landing sites for invading enemy aircraft were covered with obstructions like these concrete tunnels.

Opposite page top: A scene in Hampstead in the first week of the war.

Opposite page bottom left: 'Women residents of the Royal Borough of Kensington helping with the important job of sandbag filling.'

Opposite page bottom right: ARP. Air Raid Protection plans were already in place before the war started and although wardens were both male and female, they were not all as glamorous as this.

REPORTING FOR DUTY

Opposite page: 'A scout reports to an ARP station for duty as a messenger. He cycles around with important messages carried in his stocking.'

Top left: In the early weeks of the war workmen were employed sandbagging public buildings as here at Southwark Town Hall.

Middle left: The owner of this restaurant was taking no chances. Sandbags were a way to protect against the damage caused by shock waves from a blast. Shopfronts with their vast expanses of glass were vulnerable. Many windows throughout the land were covered with a trellis-work of sticky paper to minimise the chance of flying glass.

Below: 'A busy sandbagging scene in the West End of London.'

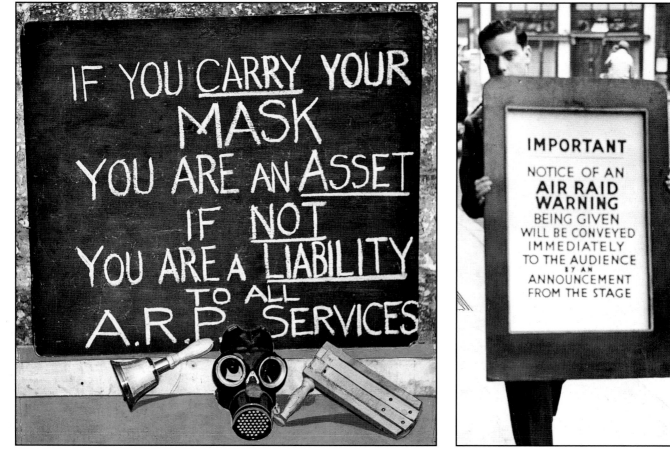

PROTECTING THE HOME FRONT 121

YOUR GAS MASK WILL PROTECT YOU

Opposite page top left: ARP wardens were responsible for ensuring strict adherence to the Blackout regulations, shelters and also for protection in the event of a possible gas attack.

Opposite page top right: 'An air-raid notice exhibited outside a West End Cinema in connection with the re-opening.' When war was declared all places of entertainment were closed down in case of bombing; within a couple of weeks many had reopened with air raid precautions in place.

Opposite page bottom left: Always carry your gas mask. 'ARP fashion in Regent St.' 3rd October 1939.

Opposite page bottom right: Walking in Hyde Park soon after the outbreak of war, these three young women all dutifully carry their masks.

Right: Shoppers going about their business in Southend prepared for a 'mock gas attack'. The Germans never made use of poison gas in any of their raids on Britain.

Below: An everyday exchange with the milkman! In this 'mock' attack in Brighton tear gas was released.

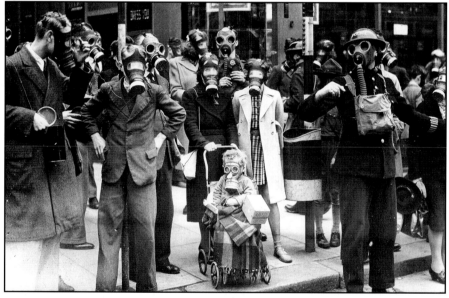

GAS ATTACK IN RICHMOND

Above: George Street in Richmond during a gas practice in May 1942. Shops on the 'gassed' side had to close while customers rushed to the safe side of the street.

Middle: A policeman directing pedestrians and traffic during the Richmond gas practice.

Bottom: Richmond less than a month later in June 1942 and no one can be seen carrying their gas mask.

Opposite page top left: And baby came too! This huge box strapped to the handles of the pram carries the respirator suit that substituted for the adult gas mask.

Opposite page top right: Customised gas-mask cases. 'Even the premier and his wife smiled when they passed these young ladies in the park yesterday, with umbrella designs on their gas-mask cases.'

Opposite page bottom: Chelsea pensioners, veterans of wars from another era, carrying their gas masks.

HOME COMFORTS

'Mr Frank Pinkerton of West Wickham has solved the problem of air raid sheltering in comfort. To his own design he has erected an air raid shelter in the lounge of his own home. The shelter which has room for six persons is built of thick concrete block, a curved roof giving great strength in case of house collapse. Fitted with bunks, carpets etc the family are enabled to sleep in security and comfort.'

Opposite page top: This notice was posted in Littlewood's store in Manchester's Piccadilly in September 1939.

Opposite page bottom left: Two young boys descend hand-in-hand into this shelter in Southwark. Adapted from the Borough Tube it was the largest air-raid shelter in Britain, able to hold 11,000 people. It had eight entrances and ranged in depth from 50 - 70 ft.

Opposite page bottom right: A much more intimate shelter near Saunderton Station in High Wycombe, this had an internal diameter of 12 ft and a height of 6 ft.

SHELTER COMFORTS

Above: A new type of bunk for the home-based Anderson shelter is demonstrated. A London policeman first designed and made them, then suggested them to the Ministry for Home Security who adopted the idea.

Left: An indoor 'table' shelter.

Opposite page: Early in the London Blitz people sought shelter in London's Tube stations. At first the authorities discouraged it, worried that the public might develop a 'deep shelter mentality' but public pressure made them relent.

ASLEEP IN THE TUBE

Londoners asleep on the escalators during September 1940.

Top right: 'The warden sees that the children are "comfy" in their hammocks at the Aldwych underground railway, now opened to the public as an official refuge.'

Middle right: Eventually bunks were installed on the platforms.

Bottom right: Passengers on the platform wait for the last train while others settle down to sleep in their bunks.

WOMEN AND CHILDREN FIRST

Above: Two women at Covent Garden read a notice appealing to men not to use the Underground as a shelter.

Top: Entrance to a public shelter in London.

Left: 'Two conflicting notices posted outside the well-sandbagged premises of a firm in the Strand are attracting the attention of passers-by. The first, put up in the name of the City of Westminster, intimates that a public air raid shelter for 150 persons is inside the building. The other notice gives the opposite view of the firm.'

WHEN THE BOMB DROPS

Left: Amid the ruins this air-raid shelter of reinforced concrete was undamaged despite being only 25 yards from where the bomb dropped. However, everyone knew that a shelter would not stand a direct hit. In one of the worst incidents of the war 110 people were killed while sheltering in, or travelling through, Bank Tube Station when it received a direct hit.

Below: Demonstrating an exit route from a cellar shelter in case of an emergency.

Dog - Owners !

You are not allowed to take your dog into a Public Air Raid Shelter—

but

BOTH YOU AND YOUR CANINE FRIEND ARE WELCOME HERE WHEN A WARNING IS GIVEN

NO RESPONSIBILITY CAN BE ACCEPTED

For Advice on any question affecting Dogs, ask
**THE
NATIONAL CANINE DEFENCE LEAGUE**
(a N.A.R.P.A.C. body)
VICTORIA STATION HOUSE, LONDON, S.W.1
(CHARLES R. JOHNS, Secretary)

H. L. Castle, Ltd., Water Lane, Watford.

PROTECTING MAN'S BEST FRIEND

Opposite page top left: This poster announces shelters where dogs and their owners can go together.

Opposite page bottom left: The owners of this home are happy to share their shelter with other dog-lovers and their pets.

Opposite page bottom right: At one of the National ARP centres for animals, an injured dog is treated.

Opposite page top right: A dog is removed on a stretcher from a bombed building by members of the People's Dispensary for Sick Animals.

Below: Demonstrating aids to help people to be seen more clearly during the Blackout.

Left: Lines of communication. Two men reading one of the Ministry of Information's regional bulletins in a London suburb.

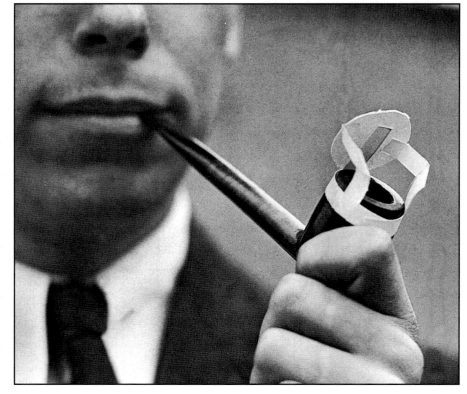

BLACKOUT

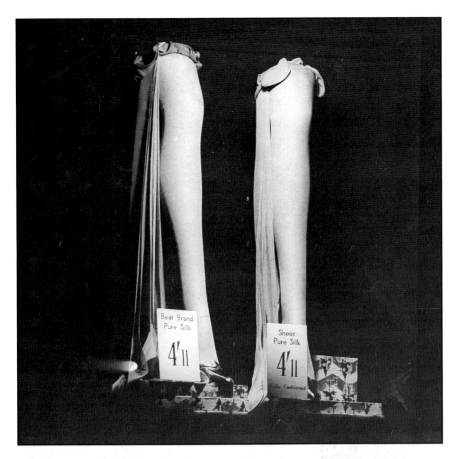

Opposite page top: A red torch held by a policeman shining through the Blackout to pull up any motorist caught exceeding the newly established 20 mph speed limit in built-up areas.

Opposite page bottom left: A car headlamp mask to dim and divert the light downwards.

Opposite page bottom right: Sometimes the Blackout was carried to extreme. This is a 'pipe-smoker's shield - at each pull the glow from the pipe is reflected forward.'

Left: Official shop lights for window displays.

Below: A candlelight service at Christ Church, West Green, Tottenham in response to the Blackout regulations. All buildings were required to conform and in the early weeks of the war Blackout materials sold out rapidly.

DIMOUT

'Tottenham Court Road looked almost pre-war last night when the new "maximum" lighting was switched on.'

Above: When the Blackout ended on 17th September 1944, it was replaced by the 'dimout' which allowed an increase in luminosity. Here are the new lighting regulations at Paddington.

Opposite page top: Blackpool illuminations dimout style.

Opposite page bottom: 'Manchester, Britain's brightest city.' It was the first city to change to the brighter lighting.

THE ENEMY WITHIN

Opposite page top: 'A detective escorts a woman from the Fascists' headquarters in Westminster - one of the officials taken to the "Yard". Note her "lightning" badge.'

Opposite page bottom left: Police take away documents and files during this raid on the headquarters of the British Union of Fascists in May 1940. In July of the same year it was officially banned.

Opposite page bottom right: Crowds look on as the Fascists are taken away by police.

Left: This armed guard at Folkestone Harbour is awaiting the return from Germany of Unity Mitford. A devoted admirer of Hitler, she became known as the 'Storm Troop Maiden'.

Below left: Police checking identity papers in a bar in the West End.

Below right: Checking travellers at a South Coast railway station. In April 1944 visitors were banned from going within 10 miles of the coast from the Wash to Land's End as the Allies prepared for the invasion of Europe.

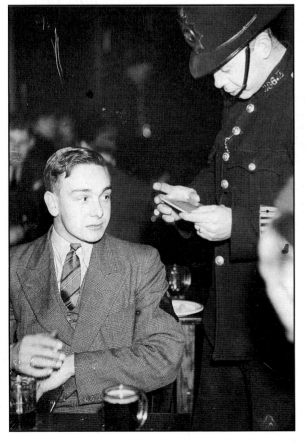

PLEASE HAVE IDENTITY CARDS READY FOR INSPECTION

BLACK MARKET

Above: Two American soldiers are approached by Black Marketeers at Rainbow Corner, Shaftesbury Avenue. 'They weren't interested.'

Above right: In another transaction a wrist-watch is valued. The police had a constant battle with Black Marketeers, many of whom were on the wrong side of the law before the war started.

Right: Money changes hands. Shop prices were strictly controlled, as was the amount that could be bought. Unrationed goods would often be kept 'under the counter' to be sold at the controlled price to regular customers. Black Marketeers, however, obtained their goods in questionable ways and sold them to the highest bidder.

OLDHAM IN THE FIRING LINE

Above: 'Oldham Police war Reserves receiving rifle instruction under the supervision of Detective Sergeant H. Smith, and squad commander A. Travers.'

Left: 'Bren gunners in action against low-flying enemy aircraft.'

Below: An air sentry receives the message 'enemy planes approaching'.

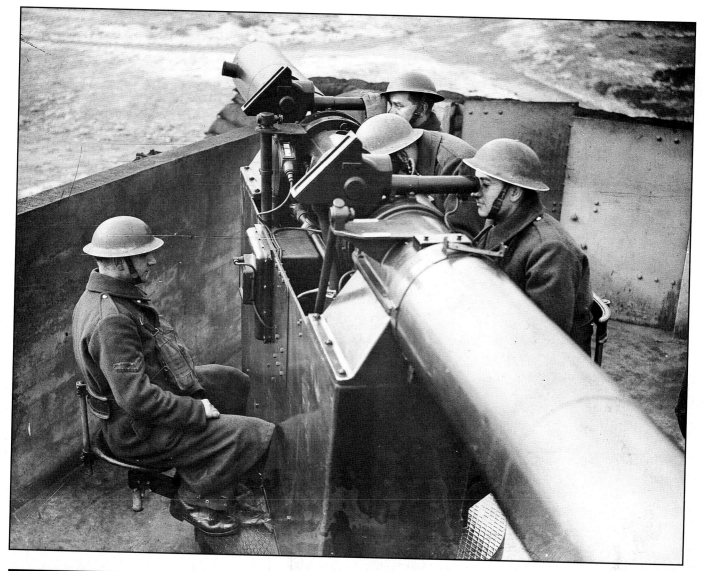

GUNNING FOR THE LUFTWAFFE

Opposite page top: Bringing the gun into action and following the target at an anti-aircraft unit somewhere in the North.

Opposite page bottom left: Manning a machine gun.

Opposite page bottom right: Taking aim at low-flying enemy aircraft.

Above: Using the height-finding apparatus to help target the guns.

Left: Loading the gun with anti-aircraft shells.

KEEPING THE SNEAK-RAIDER AT BAY

Left: 'Coast Bofors gun in action against sneak raiders.' By May 1943 when this photograph was taken there were very few air raids - only the occasional opportunistic raid trying to pierce the defences which by this stage were effective and efficient, but it meant that the gunners had to maintain a constant alertness.

Below: A year later and the same gunners are a first line of defence against the flying bombs, a new and terrifying weapon which could penetrate as far as the outskirts of North London, without risking the life of a Luftwaffe pilot.

Opposite page top: 'Gunner Brachin on the job.'

Opposite page below: 'Bob Harrison gives the order to fire.'

EYES OF THE RAF

Left: Gunner Carson loading shells.

Below: Anti-aircraft units relied on the men and women of the Observer Corps to signal the approach of enemy aircraft. The Corps was a civilian organisation, operationally controlled by Fighter Command. Full-time members worked 48 hours per week but many were part-time, taking on shifts in addition to their other jobs.

Opposite page top: 'An observer identifies a plane while his colleague plots the course.'

Opposite page below: Dawn breaks on an Observer Corps listening post.

PARTNERS IN THE CORPS

Left: Mrs Schofield and Mrs Fenwick, members of the Observer Corps studying aircraft.

Below: 'Mrs Schofield is relieved at her post by her husband, also a Corps member, despite a full-time job as a draughtsman.'

THEY ASKED TO BE GASSED

Left: Volunteers at the London Homeopathic Hospital were 'blistered' by mustard gas in order to monitor the effects and possible remedies.

Below: A doctor and an ARP worker demonstrate how to apply a tourniquet during this lecture on First Aid at the Westminster Hospital in June 1940. The event was so popular hundreds of people had to be turned away.

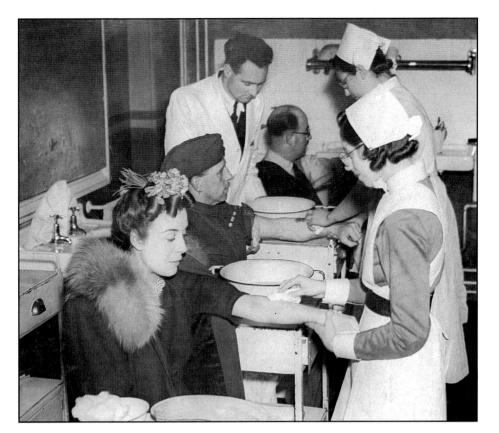

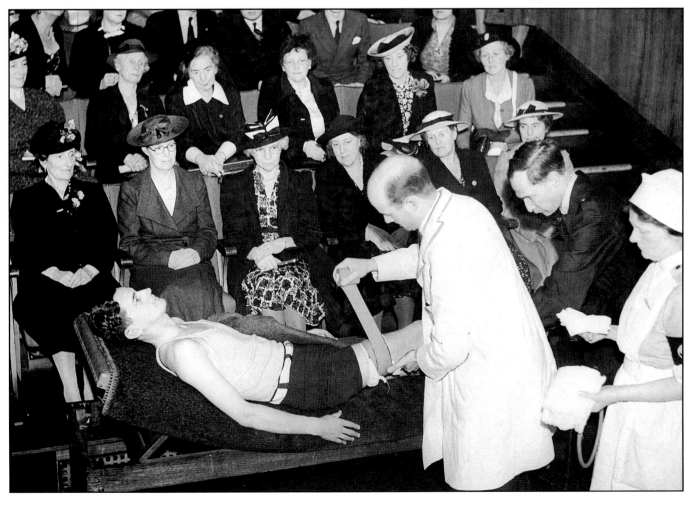

ROOF SPOTTERS

Above: All factories and institutions had their own roof spotters, usually members of staff who did an extra shift. The roof spotter's job was to act as an early warning to those inside the building of the approach of a raid. Here the roof spotter works on while West Ham play Chelsea in December 1940, at the height of the Blitz. The gate was less than 2,000.

Left: Keeping their eyes peeled on the top of the Daily Mail building, with St Paul's in the background.

Opposite page top: Roof spotters receiving training in aircraft recognition from an RAF officer.

Opposite page bottom: 'An RAF officer pointing out a British type of plane overhead.'

GET FIT FOR SERVICE

Opposite page: 'Off on a recruiting drive complete with civilian and military instructors and banner.' Part of a scheme, post-Dunkirk, to encourage men to get themselves fit to join the military or home defence units.

Left: 'The first official broomsticks.' Arms drill at the Empire Stadium, Wembley, using ash sticks which weighed approximately the same as a service rifle.

Below: 'There was a good muster of volunteers of all ages at the Bradford Park Avenue Football Ground today (Saturday, 22nd June 1940) to take part in the "Fitness For Service" Drills organised by the Central Council of Recreative Physical Training. The men take part in all kinds of drills and recreative games and also receive instruction in boxing.'

Bottom: Resistance training!

DAD'S ARMY

Opposite page: A veteran of the Great War in uniform again as an LDV. This is the classic image of the Home Guard, dubbed 'Dad's Army'.

Above: Men of the Home Guard parade in Piccadilly Circus in May 1944. By this time they are indistinguishable from the military soldier.

Top left: When first formed the Home Guard was called the Local Defence Volunteer force. These men parading in June 1940 wear LDV armbands. A call had gone out as the Germans were rapidly advancing in France, to all men 'not presently engaged in military service between the ages of 17 and 65' to volunteer to help fight off an invasion. In the first week quarter of a million volunteered and women also joined up.

Bottom left: Some of the earliest LDVs marching through London's streets. Major General Cecil Pereira takes the salute.

JOINING UP

Left: Queuing to join the parachute defence corps at Loughton in Essex. There was a need for many specialist units as the Home Guard increasingly took over duties normally undertaken by regular soldiers.

Below: August 1940, making 'Molotov Cocktails which have been adopted for use by the Home Guard. They are considered even more effective than hand grenades against armoured divisions.'

Opposite page top: It was Churchill's idea to change the name from LDVs to Home Guard and from 23rd July this is how they were known. Here is the Daily Mail's Home Guard unit on parade. Early problems with uniforms and equipment were overcome and by 1941 the Home Guard was well equipped and trained.

Opposite page bottom: Being inspected by Viscount Rothermere, owner of the Daily Mail.

PARLIAMENTARY HOME GUARD

With an HQ in Westminster Hall this unit comprised members of both Houses, staff and officials from the building and members of the Press. This picture shows Lord Strabolgi on duty in the snow in Palace Yard.

Opposite page top: The King inspecting the Home Guard at Worcester Park.

Opposite page bottom: Home Guard marching in to take the guard at Buckingham Palace.

THEY'RE CHANGING GUARDS AT BUCKINGHAM PALACE

Top: Increasingly the Home Guard took over guarding key sites. Here the 1st County London (Westminster) Battalion, take on guard duties at Buckingham Palace.

Left: Certificate issued to the 1,701,208 men and 31,824 women who had served their country in the Home Guard.

Below: Home Guard in their final parade before being disbanded in November 1944.

Opposite page: Posting sentries at Buckingham Palace.

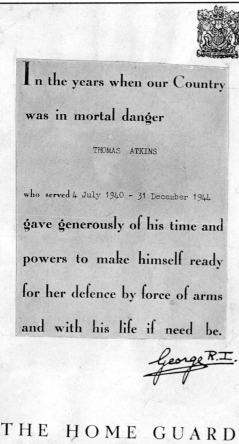

In the years when our Country was in mortal danger

THOMAS ATKINS

who served 4 July 1940 – 31 December 1944

gave generously of his time and powers to make himself ready for her defence by force of arms and with his life if need be.

George R.I.

THE HOME GUARD

FULL BLAST IN WOLVERHAMPTON

Above: Wolverhampton Auxiliary Fire Service demonstrates the effectiveness of 100 hoses at full blast.

Left: During the second Fire of London the fire-fighters of London had their most demanding challenge. Here they are trying to prevent the spread of the fire beneath St Paul's.

Opposite page top: 'Some of the men whom London must praise at work this morning.' (30th December 1940)

Opposite page bottom: The morning after. Fire crews, after fighting the blaze all night, have to clear up their equipment.

FIREFIGHTERS AT WORK

Opposite page top: Filling cans with petrol to fuel the pumps which help raise the water pressure for the fire hoses.

Opposite page bottom: A lone fireman damping down the smouldering embers of a fire.

Left: This woman fireguard waits for orders from a comrade who is fighting the flames from a balcony.

Above: Firemen playing their hoses on a fire caused by an incendiary device.

Below: Clearing up while colleagues remain at work damping down burnt-out buildings in Fore Street.

A WELL-EARNED CUPPA

Opposite page top: A welcome break and a cup of tea.

Opposite page bottom: The Salvation Army offers tea to the firefighters. There were many organisations, run by volunteers, which provided refreshments for those on duty or caught in air raids.

Top: Rescue operations were carried out by a whole series of organisations. There were ARP personnel and the Heavy Rescue brigade required when there was any heavy lifting to be done, but often the military and police as well as civilians also helped. In this rescue in Folkstone after a V2 attack American soldiers, Home Guard and British sailors are all involved.

Left: Making safe. The Royal Engineers' expertise with explosives was important in making safe many dangerous structures. Engineers laid charges which simply demolished anything unsafe.

DEMOLISHING THE DANGER

Top left: 'R.E. s laying a gun cotton charge ready for demolishing a dangerous wall in the city.'

Left: These Royal Engineers are working among the ruined buildings of the City of London in the week following the Fire of London.

Above: Demolition squads working on a damaged bank.

Right: The demolition squad at work on a bombed house - one of the gang is working at the end of a rope making the roof safe. In the foreground another man works on a street lamp, many of which were still gas at this time.

Chapter Four

IN UNIFORM

It is noticeable that in many of the photographs taken during the war, either for the public archive or for personal memories, there is someone in uniform. Military forces were stationed on bases throughout the country but did get out to mix with the civilian population, either helping with the war effort or socialising. Many RAF aircrews were stationed for the duration in Britain; army soldiers spent many months in the country before being shipped out as the fighting fronts opened up; and the navy's sailors spent long stretches at sea before earning home leave. Soldiers, sailors and airmen from a variety of Allied Forces, from the Free French to troops from British colonies to the Americans were to be seen in uniform around the country. There were also around half a million women in the British Forces, most of whom served in Britain. Apart from the Military, there were a whole host of civilian groups who spent at least part of their time in uniform - ARP wardens, the Home Guard, Fire-Fighters, the Observer Corps, the Voluntary Ambulance Service, to name but a few.

With the declaration of war there was an immediate need for fighting men. They came from several sources - there were the regular members of the armed forces, members of Territorial or reserve forces, those who volunteered with the declaration, and those who were conscripted. A Conscription Bill had been introduced in May 1939 and soon afterwards all young men under 21 were registered, ready to be called up whenever needed. As the war progressed the age for conscription widened to include men between 18 and 50, and also

single women between the ages of 20 and 30. Most conscripted men were sent into the army and by June 1941 two and a quarter million were in the service.

The majority of the men evacuated from the beaches at Dunkirk were regular or reserve army soldiers, as by that time few of the conscripted men had completed their training. While Dunkirk was a triumph in that it rescued the men, most of the army's equipment was left behind, leaving a trained force without the equipment to retake what was by now a 'fortress' Europe. For much of the next year there were millions of soldiers stationed all over Britain, waiting for replacements and additions to the equipment and weapons lost in May and June 1940, waiting for the call to fight.

Many of these soldiers stationed throughout the country were a useful supply of manpower to help with harvests and many other projects, from fortifying the beaches to guarding sensitive installations. They also helped fight fires and repair bomb damage during and after air raids. Thus soldiers were seen out and about, becoming important members of the community in which they were stationed.

The most glamorous uniforms were those of the RAF. Not only were they more attractive in cut and colour, they were associated with a force which had connotations of danger, heroism and romance. In 1939 the RAF was only 21 years old, having been formed at the end of the First World War from the Royal Flying Corps, when air warfare was in its infancy. It was a

Women recruits to 'NAAFI' (Navy, Army and Air Force Institutes) being drilled by an army sergeant at their base in Watford.

young service and many of the men were also young. It was dangerous – 150,000 men of a total of around 600,000 were killed during the war. It was the service which became the front line in the Battle of Britain after the army's retreat from Dunkirk, the service which scored the first notable victory against the enemy.

During the 'phoney war' the service which saw the greatest loss of life was the navy. British ships were assigned to protect the essential supplies of food and raw materials carried across the Atlantic from the USA by the British merchant fleet; they were also involved in battles for superiority at sea, especially in the war in the Pacific. One of the biggest threats to shipping was from U-boats. At the beginning of the war the German navy had only twenty-eight U-boats; their success in sinking supply ships encouraged the building of more. Convoys of ships, protected by warships were harried by groups

of U-boats nicknamed 'wolf packs'. Later in the war British convoys braved the freezing conditions of the North-west passage to supply the USSR. There were also supply convoys to the island of Malta which was virtually under siege for four months.

Each of the three services had their female auxiliary corps. After the First World War the Women's Royal Naval Service (WRNS or Wrens) and the Women's Auxiliary Air Force (WAAF) had been disbanded. Both corps were re-formed in April 1939. The Auxiliary Territorial Service (ATS) had continued between the wars as a reserve of trained women to assist the army in the event of war. There were also a number of smaller women's corps which undertook specific duties – for example the Voluntary Aid Detachment (VAD) nurses and the Air Transport Auxiliary Service whose female pilots delivered planes and essential supplies.

Of course the military uniforms that could be seen around Britain during the war were not always those of the British forces. Many French troops had been rescued from the beaches in France in 1940 and they joined a growing band of military groups like the remnants of the Polish military who had managed to escape Hitler's blitzkreig and had set up bases in Britain. Until the arrival of the American GIs in January 1942, the largest contingents of foreign soldiers stationed in Britain came from the British colonies.

Uniforms in military forces provide practical clothing for the particular functions the wearer is required to undertake; a uniform also protects and aids the safety of the wearer while helping to build a sense of unity and team spirit by making the wearer identifiable to others within and outside the unit. The same is true for civilian uniforms and the outbreak of war necessitated a number of forces, often volunteer, in addition to the peacetime uniformed services, such as Fire, Police and Ambulance. The ARP Service, the Home Guard and the Women's Land Army are examples of groups formed specially to respond to wartime difficulties, while the Auxiliary Fire Service and the Police Reserve were needed to add to the peacetime numbers required through extra workload and loss of manpower.

Throughout 1944, 1945 and 1946 there was a gradual demobilisation of all the uniformed corps. The Home Guard was disbanded in November 1944. Following on from Victory in Europe in May 1945 a million men and women were demobilised from the Armed Forces and many of the other civilian volunteer forces such as the ARP Service were stood down permanently. After VJ day demobilisation of the forces continued, but it was a huge undertaking. There had been over five million people in military service at the peak of wartime need and some had to wait until 1947 to be demobbed. And of course with demobilisation came the start of National Service which was in effect an extension of the conscription introduced in 1939, but in this case it only required young men of 18 to serve for two years.

Demobilisation meant a return to peacetime, for most a return to their families and communities, a return to their former occupations, or in some case new careers. It also meant having to think more carefully about clothes and the everyday necessities that the military had often taken care of. All demobilised military personnel were given an outfit of clothes - the famous 'demob suit' – and lessons on civilian life to help them cope both practically and emotionally with the return to 'civvy street'.

June 1945, after VE Day and these British soldiers and their kit are being airlifted by the RAF to the Far East to supplement the troops transported by sea.

ON LEAVE

Opposite page top: Sailors starting
their leave in October 1939 with a
long smoke, in this case emulating
the First Lord of the Admiralty,
Winston Churchill, who was known
for his fondness for cigars.

Opposite page bottom: Members of
the ground staff of 603 (City of
Edinburgh) Fighter Squadron with
their Alsatian mascot. The crosses on
the side of the plane represent the
number of 'kills' the pilot had made.

Right: A soldier with his kitbag,
passing through London on 23rd
March 1941, dropped in to
Westminster Cathedral to join in the
service and prayers.

Below: Soldiers during the London
bus strike in 1944, here collecting
their blankets at Hammersmith
Garage before making their beds in
the buses they will run to take people
to work.

BASIC TRAINING ON THE COAST

Opposite page top: 'Our troops are constantly carrying out exercises in which they practise dealing with a force of enemy which is assumed to have landed on the coast. In this way they keep themselves fit and accustomed to the techniques of seashore fighting.'

Opposite page below: Men of the London Irish Regiment train in October 1940 with rifles and fixed bayonets to repel a coastal invasion.

Right: A member of the Royal Fusiliers at revolver practice on a South Coast beach in June 1941.

Below: August 1940 and post-Dunkirk, at the height of the Battle of Britain, troops of the Black Watch stationed on the South Coast train to repel any attempt to land German paratroopers. This unit, pictured springing into action, used bicycles for manoeuvrability and speed, enabling them to reach invaders landing in out of the way locations.

GETTING BACK TO THE FAMILY

Two British soldiers, home on leave from France, telephoning to tell those who have missed them that they are back in England and that postponed leave had been granted at last.

Opposite page top: April 1940 and a soldier is greeted by his family as he comes home on leave for ten days before returning to France.

Opposite page bottom left: This soldier is greeted by two members of his family. Unlike some of his comrades who returned earlier in February 1940, he'd had time to write home to inform them of his leave.

Opposite page bottom right: The wedding of Private George Pinnock to Miss Joan Cox on 25th April 1940 at St Stephen's Church, Rochester Row, Victoria. The groom was on a 72-hour pass from his regiment, the Highland Light Infantry, and they were to see each other just once more in the next five years.

WOUNDED IN ACTION

Above: These wounded and sick men are recuperating in Hatfield House which was taken over by the government and turned into a military hospital.

Left: A wounded soldier of the British Expeditionary Force is brought home after the first battles in the lightning strike in May 1940 which led to the retreat from Dunkirk.

Opposite page top left: A nurse lights a cigarette for a wounded soldier at a hospital in Southern England.

Opposite page top right: St Dunstan's Convalescent Home near Brighton was converted into a special hospital for those injured in the eyes. Here a soldier shares his wireless headphones with a nurse.

Opposite page below: Recuperating from injuries sustained at Dunkirk, soldiers enjoy a spot of billiards with the nurses.

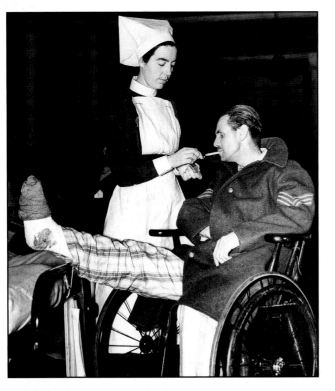

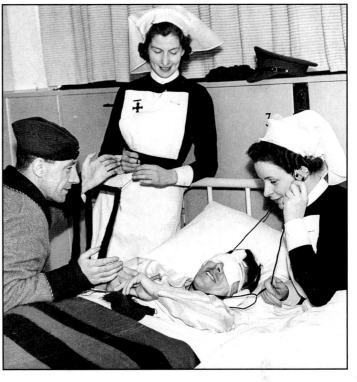

HMS VICTORY GOES BACK TO WAR

Opposite page: Nelson's old ship was pressed into service as a training ship. Here two British sailors write their letters home on the wooden deck, surrounded by the blocks and ropes of the olden days.

Left: 'Jolly Tars' of HMS Ganges take a welcome break in their training as they take their Christmas leave in 1940.

Below: 'This is the happiest picture you have seen for a long time and one which depicts the great paternal quality of our sailors. These two sailors in the cheeriest of moods, carry their babies for their wives while on their way to the station while returning from leave.'

HEROIC SURVIVORS

Left: A survivor from the cruiser 'Effingham' which was lost in Norwegian waters in June 1940, pictured passing through London on his way back to base. He is wearing a soldier's battledress but has sewn his naval insignia onto his cap and attached a badge and medal ribbon rescued from his naval uniform.

Below: These men being fitted out with new kit are survivors from the aircraft carrier 'Courageous' sunk in September 1939 in the Atlantic. Five hundred men died when 'Courageous' went down; for the first months of the war the navy was the service that bore the biggest loss of life as the German navy hunted ships at sea with their U-boats, which roamed the seas in groups called 'wolf packs', and attacked ships in their bases. Ships were also in danger from magnetic mines laid at sea and attack by aircraft.

Opposite page top: Men from the aircraft carrier 'Ark Royal', torpedoed in the Mediterranean in November 1941, arrive back in England.

Opposite page bottom: Survivors from the destroyer 'Gurkha' setting off on a well-earned leave. Attacked in the North Sea by at least 30 Dorniers the destroyer continued to fight as she went down, only breaking off as the deck went under water.

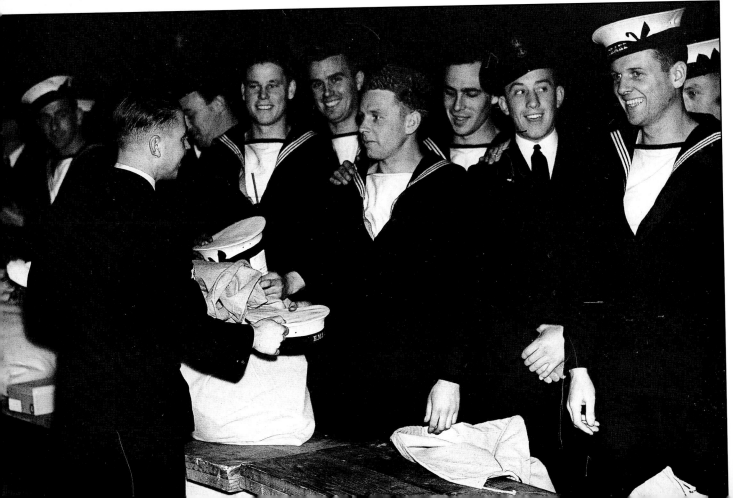

'CHEESECAKE' DIVE-BOMBER

Right: Ground crew from the navy's Fleet Air Arm at work on a new Voigt-Sikorski 'Chesapeake' dive-bomber, nicknamed the 'cheesecake' by the men. The bomber, designed and made in the USA, was made available to Britain under the Lend-Lease Agreement, made in March 1941. This allowed Britain to have equipment like this bomber and pay for it after the war.

Below: This RAF crew were pictured immediately after a huge air battle over Dover in July 1940 in which Germany attacked with 100 planes.

Opposite page: 'The crew of a bomber have a few moments rest on the tender of bombs which will shortly be loaded onto their machine, to be dropped on some specified objective in Germany'.

PREPARED FOR INSTANT ACTION

Opposite page top: RAF pilots sleep and play games in their Rest Room at their base 'somewhere in Scotland'.

Opposite page bottom: 'The men of the RAF Fighter Squadrons are ever on the alert, whether at work or during their brief hours of relaxation. This picture, taken at the County of London Squadron of the Fighter Command, shows the spirit which prevails amongst these men at all times and which has spurred them on to render their unforgettable service to their country.'

Above: Members of the Squadron listen to the account of his recent experience by a New Zealand officer who had just come in after bailing out when he was shot down. The men to whom he is recounting his tale are resting between sorties in one of the biggest battles of the Battle of Britain.

Left: RAF cyclists carrying food to feed Barrage Balloon crews. Most of the Barrage Balloon sites were without catering facilities and so food was prepared at a central depot and then transported in hay boxes which kept everything piping hot, even over distances of 10 miles.

SCRAMBLED

Opposite page: Fighter pilots rush to their planes after a warning from HQ. An unidentified plane had been reported by the Observer Corps and the planes sent up to intercept it.

Below: 'In the Operations Room of Air Defence Headquarters are the brains of the whole defence system. Here are the telephonists around the map on which they place and move models of raiders.'

Left: During his tour of Fighter Stations in June 1940, the King chatted with members of a squadron just as they were about to leave for a flight over enemy territory.

Bottom: RAF ground crews bringing in a Heinkel to a secret air base where British pilots fly captured German planes to give the Air Ministry inside information about the aircraft.

EVERYONE'S IN UNIFORM

Above: An assorted group of civil defence workers in a variety of uniforms march past the King who receives the salute at a Civil Defence Service in St Paul's.

Left: A policeman in wartime uniform. The protective tin helmet was the principal change to the police's pre-war uniform.

Opposite page top: VAD (Voluntary Aid Detachment) nurses, who served in military hospitals, greeting soldiers and their families returned from the East in April 1940 to bolster the army in Europe.

Opposite page bottom: Canadian troops take a break after acting as German air invaders in an exercise to test London's defences in July 1941. The Post Office Home Guard were the force defending London in this exercise. Troops from many British colonies supported and supplemented the home forces, many serving in the Eighth Army in North Africa.

OVER HERE!

Opposite page top: 'Doughboys', American soldiers arrive in Britain. Here is the first contingent landing in Northern Ireland after being shipped across the Atlantic.

Opposite page bottom: Irish women and children greet the first contingent of the American Expeditionary Force to land in Britain. Under the command of Major General Russell P. Hartle, they set up camp in Ulster.

Top and middle right: The first GIs landed in Northern Ireland on January 26th 1942, just seven weeks after the Japanese raid on Pearl Harbor on 7th December 1941 which drew the USA into the war. Here the troops take refreshments after landing.

Below: As they march through the streets of Northern Ireland, GIs make friends with the natives. It was the start of what was to be a complex relationship between the British population and the American soldiers.

JEEPS HIT LONDON

Opposite page top: American troops drive through London in a 'jeep', described as a 'baby reconnaisance car'.

Opposite page bottom: Getting acquainted with the pigeons in Trafalgar Square. American troops arrived in London in early March 1942 and this was clearly a useful publicity shot.

Above: Inside a hut in the Home Counties on a USA Army camp, erected to house the growing numbers of American troops stationed in Britain.

Right: 'A race for the canteen. These doughboys will be racing with even greater zest for the "second front" one day.' This picture was taken in June 1942; it was to be a further two years before the 'second front' would open up.

LENDING A HELPING HAND

Left: American troops helping to construct, on this bomb site, emergency housing for Londoners bombed out of their homes.

Bottom left: Brian Lee, aged 9, gets a helping hand from an American soldier who straightens his tie before he leaves for the country in an evacuee party.

Bottom right: The US flag hangs at half mast in Shaftesbury Avenue on 13th April 1945 as a mark of respect for President Roosevelt who had died unexpectedly the day before, less than four weeks before the surrender of Germany and VE Day.

Opposite page: The landlord of a village pub serves beer to American troops stationed in the country.

MAKING FRIENDS WITH THE LOCALS

Above: Two women in Trafalgar Square are snapped by an American soldier.

Left: This American soldier cycled to Ascot and consulted one of the locals for tips about the runners.

Bottom left: Joan Clarke, of the National Fire Service, offers a light to a newly arrived American soldier, Sergeant Frank Dardanell from Verona, Pennsylvania.

Opposite page top: May 1944 and a US soldier, armed with a carbine, holds up a bus in a London street.

Opposite page bottom left: On the bus all identity papers of military personnel are examined, whether American, British or Allied.

Opposite page bottom right: 'American soldiers whose papers did not satisfy civil and military police were taken away in Army lorries.' In the run up to D-Day, it was important that all military personnel who should be involved in training and preparation for the assault on Europe were doing just that and not enjoying some 'extra leave'.

GIs ON PARADE

Left: A contingent of American troops marches along the Embankment from Westminster to Trafalgar Square on the Allied Wings for Victory Parade in March 1943.

Below: The 14th Major Port Transportation Corps of the US Army march through the ancient Bargate of Southampton with fixed bayonets and colours flying in March 1946. They were the first foreign troops to be granted this privilege because of their close association with the port during the war. Over 2,000,000 US troops embarked at Southampton.

Opposite page: 'For the first time since 1917, US troops paraded through London when they marched from Grosvenor Square to the City of London to lunch at the Guildhall with the Lord Mayor. Headed by a band, three hundred US troops and twenty marines in full ceremonial dress were cheered by London crowds along the entire route of their march.' (3rd September 1942)

IF YOU HAVE NOT SUFFERED
WILL YOU HELP THOSE WHO HAVE?
PLEASE SEND A DONATION TO THE

LORD MAYOR'S EMPIRE
AIR RAID DISTRESS FUND
MANSION HOUSE E.C.4

UNITED NATIONS

View from Buckingham Palace of the
United Nations Day Parade on 14th June
1942. The formation of the United
Nations did not come until
April 1945.

Opposite page top: Allied Forces parade
through Trafalgar Square on United
Nations Day.

Opposite page bottom: The Kings of
(l - r) Norway, Yugoslavia and Britain,
take the salute on United Nations Day.

THANKSGIVING WEEK

Top left: Starting with a service in Westminster Abbey a week of Thanksgiving for the Victory began on 16th September 1945. The date coincided with the fifth anniversary of the Battle of Britain and here the pilots and crews of the RAF lead the procession down the Mall to the Abbey.

Middle left: Royal Marine Commandos parade through Trafalgar Square during Thanksgiving week.

Bottom: On Monday 17th September the Thanksgiving parades continued. Here the Airborne troops who dropped on Arnhem in September 1944 in an attempt to take the bridge and cut off German supply lines march past.

Opposite page top: 'The great Battle of Britain fly-past.' Squadrons in formation tear across the skyline of London.

Opposite page bottom: The fly-past reaches Trafalgar Square - in the foreground is a defused V2 rocket bomb and behind that the spire of St Martin-in-the-Fields church.

SING AS YOU WAVE ME GOODBYE

Above: 'Miss Paddy Prior, one of the ENSA entertainers, amongst the troops as she sings a popular song.'

Right: 'It's a long, long way - to wherever these troops are being sent when they leave for overseas shortly, but yesterday they were having the time of their lives at an open-air concert party.' This picture, with Paddy Prior singing, was taken on Sunday 8th October 1939, a couple of days before the British Expeditionary Force embarked for France.

Above: A scene from the RAF's musical play 'Seven boys leave with Cinderfella' at the Wintergarden Theatre.

Top left: Sunday 8th October 1939 and the troops add their own talents to an open air concert before they are shipped overseas.

Middle left: 'The army of today's all right. First-class entertainment, and an all-star show at that. The ATS girls were mingling with anti-aircraft gunners - men from lonely stations over Britain - at Drury Lane yesterday (27th March 1940), watching a special performance arranged by NAAFI.'

Bottom left: The audience applaud Jack Hylton's Band playing at the Royal Artillery Theatre in Woolwich.

LAUGHTER CURE-ALL

Above: Actress Zoe Gail hands round buns in the interval of a comedy performed for injured soldiers. Jack Humphries, in the head bandage, had broken his neck in October 1944 when his lorry overturned near Amiens. He said that the laughter and enjoyment was the best medicine he'd had.

Left: 'Several hundred soldiers wounded in the "big show" saw "The Last of Mrs Cheyney" at London's Savoy Theatre yesterday (5th February 1945). Here are some of those who could walk finding a short cut from the Strand down Carting Lane.'

Opposite page: Serving soldiers take to the stage to put on a show for their fellows.

CRAZY GANG KEEP TROOPS SMILING

Opposite page top: The Crazy Gang, one of the most popular comedy teams of the war, keep these troops entertained at the London Palladium.

Opposite page bottom: Lance-Corporal Peter Mather was released from duty to stage-manage a performance of 'The Women' at Golders Green Hippodrome in November 1939. The theatre and the production had been closed down at the start of the war but this was a special performance for the Queen's Westminsters, the Lance-Corporal's regiment.

Left: A small section of the audience of 1,500 Guards who enjoyed a performance of 'Shepherd's Pie' in April 1940.

Below: Soldiers form the audience of a concert in the YMCA canteen at Waterloo Station given by station staff.

FOOTBALL FANS

Opposite page top: 'A scene at Upton Park where West Ham United played Leicester City showing the usual football fans watching the game - in Army uniform.' This picture was taken the day before war was declared and emphasises the degree to which the war was becoming inevitable.

Opposite page bottom: RAF men in France at New Year 1940 receive games equipment - footballs, quoits and boxing gloves. There was a necessity for games equipment for all the Forces at this time as there was very little action on the fighting front and the men had to occupy themselves, aside from training and waiting.

Left: Loading up cinema equipment for RAF crews stationed overseas - another way to pass the waiting time during the 'phoney war'.

Below: Dance halls became very popular. It was a place for young men and women to meet, make contact with one another and listen to popular band music. When the American GIs arrived they brought with them new music and dances like the jitterbug.

THE BOYS TO ENTERTAIN YOU

Opposite page, top and bottom: The Forces often put on entertainments for the public, frequently as part of savings drives. Here the band of the Grenadier Guards performs in Trafalgar Square to a huge crowd.

Right: The Guards band playing on top of an air raid shelter in Trafalgar Square while the youngster in the foreground plays in the empty fountain pool.

Below: 'The find of his lifetime. The band had gone and left their instruments in the roadway. In the background a soldier kept the crowd at a distance - but the little boy stepped in where grown-ups fear to tread.' These instruments were left behind by the 3rd Division of the Royal Canadian Army Corps.

Chapter Five

WOMEN IN THE WORKFORCE

'Women of Britain – come into the factories', so ran a slogan on one of the most well known propaganda posters of the war. When the war started there was a necessity for labour on all fronts. Most immediately there was a need for men to join the military but there was also a need to keep essential services, like power and transport, running and a need to produce the hardware necessary to fight the war. There were innumerable other jobs created by the war, from ARP wardens to demolition crews. Other jobs, like those in the fire service, required an increase in numbers. By 1940 Britain had three and a half million men in the armed forces. Nearly all of them had left a job behind and women were the only pool of labour from which to recruit.

The majority of women in Britain in the pre-war years had no paid employment. Many women left the parental home, married and went to live with their husbands without ever having a paid job. The vast majority of women who did work outside the home left as soon as they married – often employers had bars against employing married women. Social pressure during the depression of the thirties reinforced this convention – jobs were for men who were the 'bread-winners' in the family.

It was into this culture that, in January 1940, Winston Churchill, then First Lord of the Admiralty and a member of the war cabinet, called for a million women to help with war work, chiefly in the making of munitions. This was only one of many calls for women

workers up until December 1941 when women described as 'mobile', that is they had no pressing responsibilities in the home, aged 20 to 30, were conscripted to do essential war work, either in the forces or in industry. Throughout the war the ages for conscription were extended so that by 1943 nine out of ten single women and eight out of ten married women with children over the age of fourteen were either in the forces or in 'essential work'. Many thousands more women classed as 'immobile' took on part-time jobs outside the home or became outworkers, making or assembling small machine parts at home.

'Essential work' covered a variety of jobs. Munitions production was obviously a priority. As many of their mothers had done in the First World War, women took on jobs they had not previously been thought capable of doing. Women in this war were involved in a good deal of 'heavy' work: building ships, tanks, aircraft, barrage balloons and in fact generally extending the boundaries of what women could do even beyond those set by women in the First World War.

Munitions production included not only the building of war machines but also the manufacture of bombs, shells, mines and bullets used by those machines. Many women were employed in producing the casings for such items which involved working with smelting furnaces and hot metal. The casings were then sent to be filled in other factories, usually sited out of town because of the risk of explosion. Women working with explosives wore a cloak and beret of undyed silk, rubber

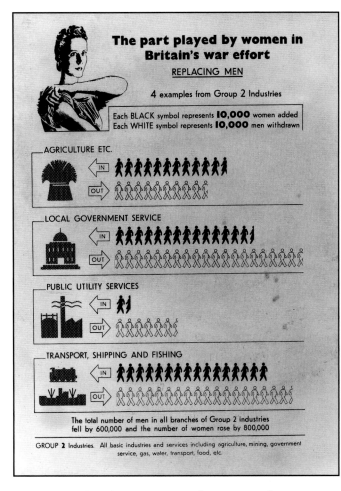

The part played by women in Britain's war effort
REPLACING MEN
4 examples from Group 2 Industries

Each BLACK symbol represents **10,000** women added
Each WHITE symbol represents **10,000** men withdrawn

AGRICULTURE ETC.

LOCAL GOVERNMENT SERVICE

PUBLIC UTILITY SERVICES

TRANSPORT, SHIPPING AND FISHING

The total number of men in all branches of Group 2 industries fell by 600,000 and the number of women rose by 800,000

GROUP 2 Industries. All basic industries and services including agriculture, mining, government service, gas, water, transport, food, etc.

What did you do in the war mummy? This picturegraph was distributed by the Ministry Of Information in 1944.

galoshes and had to remove jewellery, corsets, hairpins or anything metal which might cause a spark and set off an explosion.

Women were also needed to do many jobs essential to servicing the war industries and keeping the society running as normally as possible. Driving taxis and buses enabled people to get to their jobs. Glazing broken windows, mending roads, emptying dustbins, delivering the post were all jobs which, while not contributing directly to the war effort, helped maintain morale and made the country run smoothly.

Even though women daily proved their abilities in the workforce their pay and conditions were often very poor. They were paid considerably less than their male counterparts. The average woman's pay in 1943 was £3 2s 11d, just over 50 per cent of men's pay of £6 1s 4d.

Additionally conditions were often very basic. Safety was frequently a serious concern as factories were converted from their peacetime products and machines used for jobs they were not intended to do; other factories were hastily built or put into existing sheds and primitive buildings. Many factories were designed for men and a much smaller number of workers than those employed during the war, so that facilities like toilets and rest rooms were in short supply. Hours were long and immediately after the retreat from Dunkirk there was a need to double the production of munitions, resulting in an extension to the normal working day to 11 hours. Many women found themselves working from 8 a.m. to 7 p.m.

Food production was another area for essential work and the Women's Land Army, often nicknamed the Land Girls, formed the core of the women engaged on that. Many other women factory workers along with

'Cable-girls going overseas – new non-combatant force.' These women were employees of Cable and Wireless and were part of a new unit called 'Telecom' which was formed to aid communications from the front lines. This group were off to Malta to relieve male colleagues.

During an air raid on Dover a volunteer from the YMCA carries on serving refreshments.

school children, the forces and men in reserved occupations could take a well-earned rest by having a free holiday on a farm, providing they helped out!

Volunteering to help on the land was only one aspect of the voluntary work women were engaged in. Many women who took on essential war work jobs, part or full time, also took on voluntary work. Sometimes this took the form of office workers taking on a Sunday shift at a local factory to enable production to continue seven days a week. More usually voluntary work was organised through established groups like the Women's Institute, Women's Voluntary Service, Red Cross, Salvation Army and Church Army which were well used to helping people. These organisations provided much of the support that Social Services departments would have provided in peacetime. They offered immediate tea and sympathy to air raid victims as well as longer term support for anyone in need. Several of these voluntary bodies also organised collections of materials for the war effort, jam making and rosehip picking, as

well as promoting 'make do and mend' ideas and ways to make the most of the food rations.

Women who did 'go into the factories' or into any other work during the war found their lives burdened. Women with a home to keep found the time especially hard. Compulsory overtime meant hours were long and it was usual to work at least a half-day on Saturday. Shops were closed by the time they got home from work, so unless another family member could shop, the working housewife had to do it in her lunch hour. Queuing for everything took time and the lack of facilities for keeping food fresh meant shopping regularly. Sunday was often the only day off in which to clean the house and do the washing, usually without the benefit of any mechanical aids.

Despite the difficulties of managing a home, family and a job in which often the pay and conditions were demoralisingly low, the women of Britain responded enthusiastically to the demands the war put on them. It was often remarked how the absentee rate was lower than before the war and production rates were met in full, often by women working beyond their compulsory hours to get the job done.

KEEPING THINGS RUNNING SMOOTHLY

Above: Mrs C. Miles of Mill Hill wheeling her street-sweeping barrow. She was employed by Hendon Council to replace their male employees, many of whom, like Mrs Miles' husband were in the army.

Right: Miss Birdie Mahoney smiles as she goes about her training as a bus conductress in Cambridge.

Opposite page: Brighton trolley bus conductresses set a national record for 'regularity' – their absentee record was less than one per cent. It was estimated that on an average 8-hour shift they went up and down the bus's staircase 480 times.

ARTIST, BUTCHER, CLEANER...

Opposite page top left: 'Owing to the lack of show space due to the fact that the shop windows have been destroyed by bomb blast and are now boarded over, these girl artists were seen today putting into effect a unique idea.' The woman on the ladder is painting replicas of the goods sold in the shop onto the boards covering the broken windows.

Opposite page top right: 'A trousered girl cleaning the window of a London teashop. With many thousands of men now in the Services, a good many of their jobs have to be carried out by women.'

Opposite page bottom: 'The tricycle girls start out on a day's work.' These women are delivering towels to City offices.

Above: 'Miss Bambridge, of Coombe Hill, who is now working as a butcher at Kingston-on-Thames, is seen here serving a customer.'

Left: Offering comfort and refreshments to children being evacuated.

WOMEN WEAR
THE TROUSERS

Above: Two women model post office uniforms – the inclusion of a trousered uniform was hailed as a first.

Top: Women sorters at Mount Pleasant post office dealing with 1940's Christmas parcels.

Left: Again in 1940 a postwoman delivers the Christmas mail. Women were employed to help with the increased workload but, as this picture shows, were not given uniforms – this woman is wearing her own fashionable clothes.

Opposite page: By September 1941 many women were full employees of the post office: 'Postwomen in full uniform carrying mail bags and keys, made the afternoon collection from the post boxes in the City.'

MUNITIONS WORKERS.

Left: This young woman is one of ninety training at the Beaufoy Institute in Lambeth. She is here learning how to use measuring calipers. The women had all paid £1.2.2d (about £1.11p) for a twelve-week course.

Below: Miss Josephine De La Porte, an evacuee from Jersey, is pictured here making shells at a munitions factory in the North-East.

Opposite page top: These women are manufacturing 'Sten' guns at the Royal Ordnance factory in Theale, Berkshire.

Opposite page below: 'Girl workers in the Bottling Department showing the shells being shaped and laid out to cool.'

PROMOTING WOMEN

In January 1940 Winston Churchill, then First Lord of the Admiralty and a member of the war cabinet, called for a million women to help with war work, chiefly in the making of munitions. This picture was used to try to help promote that call – a woman works on making a shell casing at a factory in Southern England.

Opposite page top: 'The Bomb Girls. In the front rank of the "out to win the war" girls are those hard at work turning out the bombs which are being used by the RAF to give the enemy a taste of what the people of Britain have experienced. They are being turned out in all kinds of buildings, from arsenals to large sheds which have been converted into miniature factories. Ex-waitress Miss Lilian Nye hauls a 500lb bomb on a crane.'

Opposite page bottom: 'Making the gun to shoot down the hun. Girls checking cannon-shell bodies – work particularly suitable for the defter fingers of the fairer sex.'

CLOTHING
THE ARMY

Opposite page top: Supervised by a man these women are just one section of a factory where 4,500 battle-suits are completed each week.

Opposite page bottom left: Sewing soldiers' caps at a London clothing factory.

Opposite page bottom right: Studding and toe plating soldiers' boots. Millions of soldiers' boots required manufacturing or mending daily.

Right: Feeding the troops. Miss Pamela Anderson serves two ATS at a canteen for the Services in St Martin-in-the-Fields church.

Below: The NAAFI canteen at a Royal Artillery unit in Cheshire.

SHIPS AND PLANES

Opposite page: 'Women help in the high speed ship production in British shipyards. Women are now fast taking their places with the men in the yards, painting, plate marking, and generally carrying out tasks which before the war were considered hard even for the men. Miss Louisa Lines, aged 20, formerly a Yorkshire cotton machinist, painting along the scuppers of a nearly finished merchant ship.'

Left: Many women gave up peacetime occupations to go into aircraft factories. 'Mrs Eileen Glassett, a former lady sales assistant in a West End gown store, drills wing spars for the giant Halifax bomber.'

Below left: Touching up the coachwork of a plane before the engine is fitted.

Below right: Miss Elizabeth William, former radio-worker, operating a drill in an aircraft factory owned and run by mother-of-two Mrs A. Burke.

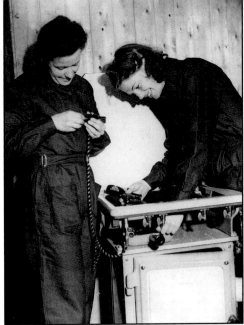

HEAVY WORK

Opposite page top: These five female demolition workers were pictured during a rest break from pulling down a bridge over the LNER line at Wembley.

Opposite page below left: 'Women in the "Pick and Shovel Brigade". At a new aerodrome somewhere in East Anglia about 100 women and girls are doing navvies' work with zest and enjoyment. Here they are laying pipes for drainage each side of the runway.'

Opposite page below right: Filling sandbags. These women were the first to be employed to clear air raid debris and help make buildings safe.

Above left: 'Mrs Flannigan, a woman bricklayer, is, with other labourers, hard at work helping to repair a Southern Railway arch in London, which was damaged during air raids on London.'

Above right: Mrs E. Knox, formerly a nurse and Mrs K. Gibbs, previously a factory hand installing a gas cooker. Women took on a whole range of jobs in the Gas Works, from gas engineers installing appliances to heavy labouring jobs filling 100-ton coke sacks or shifting red-hot coke from the retorts used to manufacture gas.

Left: 'She-navvies cheerfully wheel barrow loads of heavy stones at a railway goods yard. Women can no longer be called the "weaker sex" for all over Britain they have answered the call and taken on jobs which were previously exclusive to men. The toughest of these is surely that of "Women Navvies" a classification which includes a multitude of rough, heavy or dirty jobs.'

ON THE LAND

Left: Daisy Beales, a farmer's daughter, pictured at work on the land - here clearing land with a billhook. There was a need to reclaim land to increase production and the total arable land available increased by about 200% during the war.

Below: One of 'three girls of the Women's Land Army ploughing reclaimed land on a farm in Bedford, with the aid of three tractors working in echelon.'

Opposite page top: This Land Girl, ploughing a field in Southern England, is wearing a tin helmet to protect her from the debris as RAF fighters bring down flying bombs over open country during the summer of 1944.

Opposite page below: Margaret Gower and Mary Rigg (with 'Doodlebug' painted on her helmet) from the WLA take shelter from a battle to bring down flying bombs.

COMFORTS FOR THE TROOPS

Opposite page: 'The Shy Lovers' Post'. These women are sorting airgraph letters sent directly to London from the Provinces. The women sending them to their forces' sweethearts know that all mail is opened before being delivered and so wish to avoid the embarrassment of their passions being known locally! In this case the letters are heading for the Middle East but will all be photographed and sent on a 100 ft spool of film to minimise the weight - the film will weigh only 6 ozs while the equivalent 1500 letters without envelopes would weigh over 16 lbs.

Above: A woman dispenses articles from a 'Knitted Comforts Fund'. Knitting items for the troops was a way in which girls and women of all ages could feel they were making a contribution to the war effort.

Right: A woman voluntary worker sorts some of the hundreds of packs of playing cards, woollens and footballs sent for the men of the British Expeditionary Force - more 'comforts' for the troops.

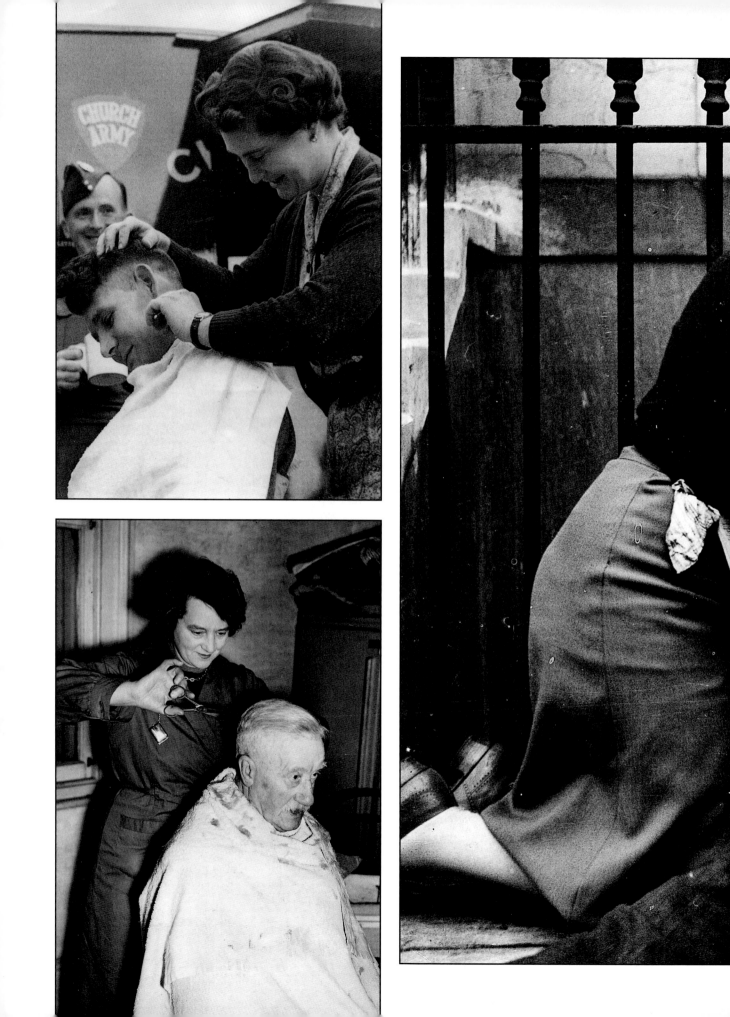

ARP DRILL

A female ARP warden attends to a minor injury during a demonstration of ARP resources and procedures.

Top left: 'Miss F. Stanley Hobart, General Montgomery's niece, drives a Church Army mobile canteen which serves troops with refreshments as well as offering military-style hair cuts.'

Bottom left: A member of the Women's Voluntary Service gives a free haircut to pensioner Mr W. H. Skipper at Woodford in Essex.

NEW ROLES

'Two more girls who give up spare time for defence work. They are Dorothy Haley Bell and Kay Astor, members of the cast of "Tony Draws a Horse", getting ready to go on duty as ambulance driver and nurse after a performance at the Comedy Theatre.'

Opposite page top: A group of volunteer ambulance women getting ready for a practice run from their station in North-West London.

Opposite page bottom: Women of the Voluntary Ambulance Service join in a military procession.

Chapter Six

DON'T YOU KNOW THERE'S A WAR ON!

Life during the war for everyone - young, old, rich, poor, male, female - was one of unremitting hard work, privation and loss in varying degrees. Any complaints about these conditions were frequently greeted with the refrain: 'Don't you know there's a war on!' The war effort took everyone's energy, be it in paid employment, service in the forces, voluntary work or running a home. Some lost homes and many had to leave their home and way of life behind. Everyone financed the war through their taxation and savings schemes which targeted all, even children. There was little to spend money on - the price of basic goods was controlled, there was not the spare manufacturing capacity in the country to produce luxury items, and imported goods put the lives of merchant seamen at risk of attack from German battleships and U-boats.

After recruiting a military force, the government's first priority was to produce the munitions with which that force could fight the war. The production of munitions needed raw materials, factory space and a labour force. Some raw materials were imported but many were provided by 'salvage'. Teams of women and children, organised by the Women's Voluntary Service (WVS), went from house to house, collecting as much metal as possible in the form of tin baths, saucepans, old tin cans, as well as scrap rubber, rags, waste paper and old animal bones.

Factory space was provided firstly by converting existing factories to munitions production. Some

factories, such as Cadbury's Chocolate and Yardley Cosmetics continued to produce some of their original products as morale boosters, but the majority of the factory was turned over to the production of weapons. Most factories converted wholly and many other buildings and premises, even large sheds, were commissioned to serve as factories for the duration of the war. This hasty conversion from their original purpose meant that conditions for the workforce were rarely anything more than basic.

With around three million working men in the forces, it was important to have enough labour to produce the weapons they needed. Men not eligible for active duty were redirected into war work and everyone that could possibly work was required to register. Both men and women were conscripted into war work, most notably the 'Bevin Boys'; from December 1943 a ballot was taken of newly conscripted men and one in ten of these men was sent to work in the coal mines. Some men, such as farmers and train drivers, came under an Essential Work Order. They were not required to undertake military service, in fact were actively discouraged, as their skills and experience were deemed to be too important to keeping the country running smoothly. These workers were not allowed to be sacked and could not move jobs, even if they wanted to.

Working hours were long. The normal working day was 8 hours Monday to Friday and 4 hours on a Saturday, but most employees worked at least a

Signing on for the 'Munition Army' at Walworth Road Labour Exchange as part of the one million men to be registered for war work.

10-hour day as they were required to do compulsory overtime. Once a work shift was over there were other demands that the war made on an individual's time. Many workers also did service with the Home Guard or the ARP service, and some people who had office jobs during the week worked in factories on Sundays to enable the factory workers to have a day off. Others 'lent a hand on the land' during their spare time, taking holidays on farms while helping planting or gathering in the harvest. Women workers also had the demands of running a home, trying to shop in their lunchtimes, cooking and cleaning in their precious hours at home.

Coping with everyday life was difficult. Food was rationed, petrol was rationed, clothes were rationed, even soap was rationed and no one was allowed to have a bath more than five inches deep. Everything that was not rationed was either in short supply or unobtainable. People had to 'make do and mend' worn or broken items and find inventive solutions to things in short supply - constructing a baby's cot out of an old drawer, experimenting with mixtures of face cream and shoe polish to colour stockingless legs, making children's clothes out of worn-out adult clothing.

Strictly controlled prices were aimed at avoiding profiteering but many shopkeepers kept unrationed items 'under the counter' to sell only to regular customers. And of course there was a black market, which was illegal and often involved those who had been on the wrong side of the law before the war.

The standard food ration was worked out by nutritionists and was a good way to ensure that the whole population were well-fed. Indeed many experts now claim that during the war people were much healthier than either before or after it. Nevertheless, it was a constant battle to obtain food. Women, in particular, had to spend hours queuing for both the ration and also for unrationed items like fresh fruit and vegetables. They also had to spend time cooking and learning to cook some of the things they would never have dreamt of serving before the war - sheep's head, carrot marmalade, fruit cakes made with dried eggs and grated beetroot, 'banana' sandwiches made from parsnips flavoured with artificial banana flavouring. Bananas were unavailable for most of the war and any oranges that were imported were reserved for children. Many people spent hours labouring in their gardens or allotments as part of the 'Dig for Victory' campaign, supplementing the family's diet with any fresh produce they could grow.

The citizens of Britain contributed to the war effort with their labour, their time, their household items, their creativity and their spirit. They also contributed to the war effort with their money. The War Budget in September 1939 raised taxation to 7/6 (37p) in every pound, raised again in 1941 to 10s (50p). Despite this tax rate, many people had money to spare; they were engaged in overtime and often a family would have at least one more income than it had before the war. However, there was little to spend it on and the government needed money to finance the war. Extra money came from people's savings. War savings were promoted endlessly, savings groups organised in factories, offices and even schools where children were encouraged to put their money into savings schemes.

By the end of the war Britain was a dull and dreary place. Six years of war had scarred many of its most beautiful buildings; people were worn out after years of hard work and worry; they wore uniforms, old, worn or 'utility' style clothing; there were shortages of even the most basic household items; and the diet, while nutritionally sound, was very limited in range. By this time everyone certainly knew 'there was a war on'!

Staff at work on the Savings Certificate Registers in the Money Order Department at the GPO (Post Office) where the savings of millions of people were administered.

PASSED UNDER WORKING CONDITION

Opposite page top: Inspecting shells at a Royal Ordnance factory. Quality control was very important as no one wanted to put the fighting men at risk from their own equipment.

Opposite page below: Inspection was carried out at all stages of the production process. Here the cases for naval shells are being checked.

Right: Storing torpedoes in an Admiralty factory ready for testing. Each torpedo contained more than 6000 parts and took several months to complete.

Below left: Men at work on building the torpedoes in the torpedo workroom.

Below right: Every torpedo was 'tried out' and 'passed under working condition' before being dispatched to a Royal Navy ship.

SHELLS

Opposite page top: Stockpiled shells.
This photograph was taken in November
1939 and they were to be sent to the
Western Front on the Belgian-French
border where the British Expeditionary
Force waited for a German offensive.

Opposite page below: In the shell
inspecting shop at an ordnance factory.

Right: Workmen stacking mass produced
anti-aircraft shells.

Below: These shells are being readied for
transfer to the filling shops. Often shells
produced in factories inside towns and
cities were sent to munitions factories
out of town to be filled with explosives.
This reduced the risk of loss of life from
explosions, caused either by enemy
bombing or by accident.

SMALL ARMS

Above left: Piling up rifles during the early months of the war to service the British Expeditionary Force which had joined with French troops to prevent any further German advances.

Above: Rifles being stacked ready for dispatch. This photograph was taken during the week of the retreat from Dunkirk. No doubt there was useful propaganda in ensuring that the public understood that, despite the fact that the soldiers had to leave most of their equipment behind, there were plenty more weapons in stock.

Left: The inspecting room of this factory which was 'working at emergency pressure, day and night, to produce small arms, spare parts and tools.' During the twenties and thirties Britain had not spent money on armaments and consequently when the war came it was a race to provide the equipment the military needed.

Opposite page: Thousands of cartridge cases ready for filling.

BUILDING A SHIP A WEEK

Opposite page top: This ship was one of the first to be built using a technique new to British shipbuilding. Using a method widely used in the USA the various parts of the ship were constructed at inland factories and then assembled on the slipway of the shipyard. This enabled the production of both warships and merchant ships to be speeded up.

Opposite page bottom: Workers constructing a bulkhead which will be hoisted into position on the ship in the background. The ship is a merchant ship, vital to keeping Britain supplied with food and materials. At this stage of the war, 1942, Britain was launching a 10,000-ton merchant ship every three weeks and this one yard had the target of constructing 16 ships in the year.

Above: Tugs pull this 8,000-ton new warship into the fitting-out basin for the final touches before it assumes active service.

Above right: Gliding down the slipway after launching is a warship which was part of Britain's one-a-week ship construction programme. As soon as it cleared the slipway the workers would have been preparing the berth for the keel-plate of the next ship.

Right: After Hitler attacked the USSR in June 1941, Britain and Russia became allies. Here the first tanks built in Britain for use on the battlefields of Russia are received by the Soviet ambassador and members of the Soviet Military Mission.

BUILDING BOMBERS

'And this is only one factory.' A production line for the Blenheim bomber 'whose speed and range have outclassed anything the Germans have.'

Top right: 'Your flying saucepan is doing just fine. The thousands of tons of aluminium pans that housewives gave up to the Ministry of Aircraft Production are making first-rate Spitfires. Smelting factories where saucepans, preserving pans and kettles are being turned into ingots for the plane factories are working at full pressure. Men, stripped to the waist, work in an atmosphere as warm as Kew Gardens' hothouse. Day and night, and through air raid warning, they shovel your household ware into furnaces and it comes out a flowing, white-hot liquid. The photo shows men stacking pure ingots of aluminium to dispatch to the Aircraft Presses.'

Below right: Anti-aircraft guns rolling off the production line in a Midlands factory.

NEWCASTLE CO-OPERATIVE SOCIETY LIMITED

Name ....

Address ....

....

Pass Book No. ....

Number in Household .... C.P.S., N/c.

	WEEK ENDING:							
	Nov. 11th	Nov. 18th	Nov. 25th	Dec. 2nd	Dec. 9th	Dec. 16th	Dec. 23rd	Dec. 30th
BUTTER.. ..								
BACON or HAM								
SUGAR								
....								
....								
....								

ON THE RATION

Opposite page top: In January 1940 the first rationing came into effect. This photograph does not represent all of the ration as fresh milk and meat were also rationed. There were other foods such as bread, fish, offal and fruit which were 'off the ration' but they were often in short supply.

Opposite page below: Throughout the war more types of food became rationed. On 8th February 1943, tinned fruit came under the 'points' system. The points system allowed people to purchase items, usually luxury items, in addition to the basic ration. It allowed some choice, tinned plums instead of tinned peaches, but restricted the number of tins any one person could purchase.

Top left: Using coupons to buy food at a Sainsbury's store. As the sign behind the shop assistant records, it was only possible to buy rationed goods in the shop with which you were registered.

Above: This 'ration book' was issued to members of the Newcastle Co-operative Society in November 1939, before official rationing came in. Clearly a response to shortages, this was a move to ration butter, bacon, ham and sugar - these were the first items to be rationed when the official system came into effect.

Left: Collating coupons to be bound into the second issue of ration books. 'Machines costing thousands of pounds were installed for the new printing. The coupons were printed on strips of paper 8 in. wide. The full run of 50,000,000 books used 35,000 miles of it.'

CUTTING COUPONS

Above: Scenes at the Fulham office where, on the day this picture was taken, all those with a surname beginning with 'A' were required to register for new ration books.

Left: 'Should ration books be perforated?' There was much debate when the books were first introduced as to whether they should have perforated sheets of coupons. Here a grocer cuts coupons from the ration book of a Miss Ella White of Baker Street.

Below: Shopkeepers had to use scissors to cut out the coupons which were about the size of a postage stamp or smaller.

USA ORANGE JUICE FOR BABY

Above: A mobile van distributing new coupon books in an attempt to relieve the congestion at the Food Office as people queue to collect them. It had the added advantage of allowing more flexibility for working people to be able to collect their coupons.

Right: Mothers receiving bottles of concentrated orange juice for their children. The juice was newly arrived from the USA as part of the Lend-Lease Agreement. This picture at Tottenham Welfare Centre was taken at the request of the USA's Department of Agriculture to promote the scheme and publicise the Americans' generosity.

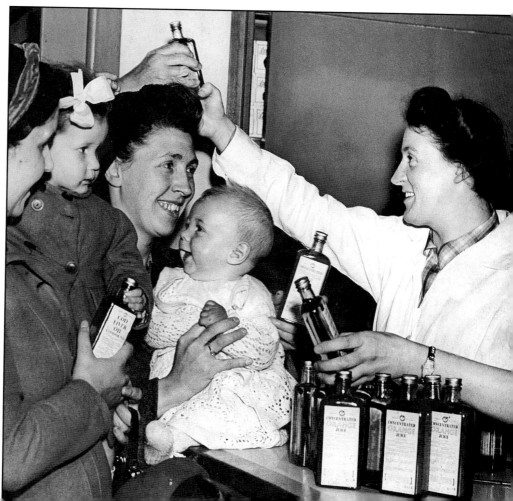

CLOTHING COUPONS

Above: By June 1941 it became necessary to ration clothing. Everyone was given 60 points a year, later reduced to 48, and could choose what to use them on. Selfridges responded to the news of clothing rationing by setting up an enquiry desk to help answer customers' queries.

Left: Buying clothes with margarine coupons! When clothes were first rationed margarine coupons could be used if the buyer had not been issued with a clothing ration book.

Opposite page top: Choosing a suit at Selfridges. The number of coupons required is displayed more prominently than the price.

Opposite page bottom: Crowds gather at the shop window to see the 'coupon cost' of clothes on the first day of the scheme.

SILK STOCKINGS

Top left: When clothes were first rationed buying 30 pairs of stockings would have used up an entire year's clothing ration.

Middle left: Prior to clothing rationing silk stockings were in short supply but this trader in Lambeth Walk has a plentiful supply of customers for his goods.

Bottom left: Women relaxing in the park while acquiring a suntan - the newly fashionable 'covering' for the legs, a replacement for stockings.

Below: An alternative method of making the legs look attractive. During the lunchtime in a City business firm one woman paints the legs of another with flesh-coloured paint, adding the finishing touch of a seam when the leg is covered.

Opposite page top: Supplies of cigarettes and tobacco were also in short supply. Selfridges had to split their permitted deliveries into smaller batches to ensure a steady service to customers and avoid selling out in a short space of time.

Opposite page below: Men queuing to buy cigarettes from a London kiosk.

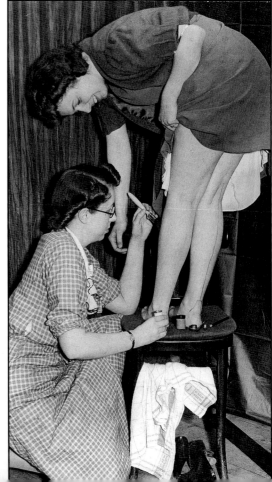

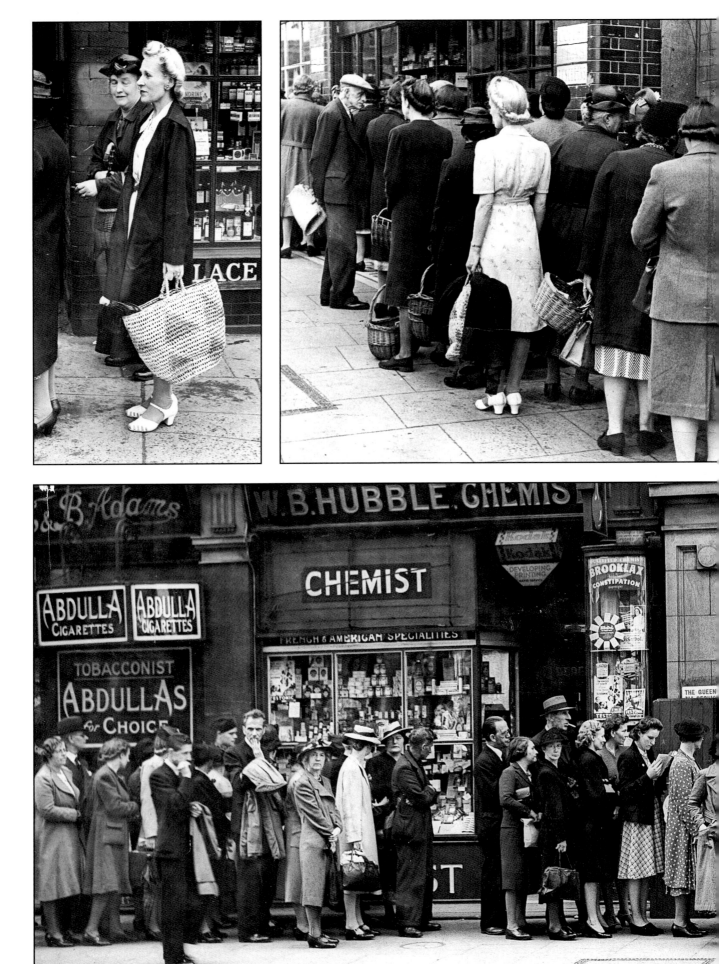

A HOUSEWIFE GOES A-QUEUING

Opposite page top left: 'At 9.00 a.m. she joins the queue for sausages. The "joint" has of course long disappeared and something must be found for lunch. The sausages are not yet in, but early queuing is necessary.'

Opposite page top right: '9.15. It's stopped raining, but it's hot and the very "flat" atmosphere is very tiring, so her coat comes off; something more to carry on her arms.'

Opposite page bottom: This queue in July 1942 formed outside a sweet shop near Leicester Square as people tried to stock up before sweets became rationed.

Above: Queue in Kentish Town for the greengrocer's. Even though this was taken in July 1945 when the victory in Europe had been won, there was no sign of an improvement in supplies.

Above right: This fishmonger has a simple way to prevent shoppers wasting time queuing. He simply informs them of what is not in stock.

Middle right: Queuing for fish in Streatham High Road in July 1945.

Bottom right: A fish queue in Hammersmith in June 1945. While the fishmonger was able to supply fish, the shop did not have any paper in which to wrap it, customers had to bring their own.

QUEUES FOR ICE CREAM AND TOMATOES

Opposite page top: This is a queue for ice cream, a luxury item, although the product these women are queuing for probably contained no cream, being made from dried milk powder, dried egg, water and flavourings. The energy required to freeze it would be sufficient to make it a luxury.

Opposite page bottom: Queuing for tomatoes at a Birmingham greengrocer's. This is again after VE Day and there was a growing movement to try to do something about the endless queuing.

Right: Women from the Salvation Army make notes at an 'anti-queue' meeting in the Waldorf Hotel between the National Council for Women and the Council of Retail Distributors.

Above: Queuing for essentials in Coventry. A week after the devastating raid in November 1940, people queue for water from a standpipe.

BOMBED OUT!

Left: An emergency 'Food Office' for those whose homes suffered damage in raids by V1 bombs in Southern England. At this office people who had lost ration books and coupons in the raids could be given replacements.

Above: A mobile unit from the National Emergency Washing Service providing free clothes washing for families who had been bombed out or those who had been moved to safer areas and did not have access to washing facilities.

Opposite page top: 'A Ministry of Food "Flying Squad" at work soon after a "flying bomb" had fallen in Southern England. A Marquee and field kitchen were set up for supplying hot meals.'

Opposite page bottom: A gift from the car magnate Henry Ford - emergency food vans which toured the bombed areas dispensing cooked food.

TRAVEL AND TRANSPORT

Left: In the early weeks of the war this garage proprietor ensured the petrol supplies were safe from the bombing with a liberal stacking of sandbags.

Above: Petrol was rationed almost immediately the war started. It was only available to members of the public for 'essential' journeys, a doctor doing his rounds in a rural area for example. Most car owners could not get petrol for their cars and in effect they were out of action for the duration of the war.

Below: A 10.00 p.m. curfew was imposed on London's buses, apart from a few buses which would run for late-night workers. This was principally to help preserve lives during the Blitz but had the added advantage of saving fuel.

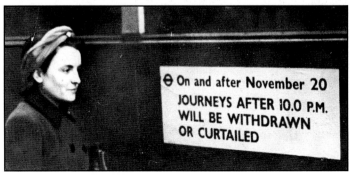

HORSE POWER

Above: An old fashioned 'growler' cab, driven by horse power, made an appearance on London's streets in response to the lack of petrol for motorised taxis.

Left: Increasing numbers of horses were seen on Britain's roads for all manner of jobs, mainly transporting goods.

Opposite page top: 'With petrol rationing and motorists laying up their cars, horses are coming into their own again. And street scenes resembling more and more those of days gone by. Compare this picture in Piccadilly yesterday (5th October 1939) with the scene in 1891 (inset right).'

Opposite page below: 'First day of petrol rationing (25th September 1939) – and this was the scene yesterday on a by-pass road near London which is usually crowded with speeding cars. People ambled pleasantly on horseback or bicycled gaily by, but for the greater part of the day there was not a car to be seen.'

FUEL SUPPLIES

Above: Coal was the most essential fuel during the war. It powered the electricity stations, was important in the production of gas, was needed for smelting metal for munitions and was the chief source of domestic heating. Ensuring supplies of coal throughout the war was always a problem. Here Marylebone Borough Council store coal for the winter at a bomb damage site in Baker Street. Keeping supplies close to the area they were needed helped to avoid congestion on the rail network at peak times of demand.

Left: Residents of an area could visit the coal stores, or dumps, pay for the coal they required and take it away with them.

Opposite page: This notice informs residents that, due to a shortage of coal in Southern England, the emergency coal dumps would be closed down.

EVERY OUNCE COUNTS

Left: 'Westminster City Council have put galvanised bins at street corners. Notices on the covers tell housewives what they should put in the bins to help feed pigs and other livestock on our farms.'

Opposite page right: Women's Land Army feeding pigs. The Women's Land Army was formed in response to the shortage of 100,000 farm labourers and the need for Britain to produce more of its food at home.

Opposite page middle and bottom left: Women of the Land Army stooking the sheaves on a farm in Buckinghamshire in the summer of 1944. In this year the WLA was 80,000 strong.

Opposite page right: Land Girls, the name women from the Women's Land Army were most frequently called, making hay on Arlington Manor Farm, Guildford, in the summer of 1942.

LEND A HAND ON THE LAND

Left: Many people were encouraged to 'Lend a hand on the land' - parties of school children, evacuees, those who wanted a 'holiday' away from the towns and cities. Here soldiers help gather the harvest in 1941, a time when there was little active fighting to be done, as Britain gathered its forces, arming and training troops for an invasion of Hitler's 'Fortress Europe'.

Below: Children evacuated to South Wales help with the potato harvest.

Right: 'Peckham Health Centre has been evacuated to the Centre's Home Farm at Bromley Common. They have taken their babies (under five years of age) with them and have taken enthusiastically to the farm life, adopting breeches, lumber jackets and top boots.'

DIG FOR VICTORY

Left: The development of allotments was also encouraged and parks and open spaces were turned over to growing food. Golf clubs, tennis courts, grass verges, the moat of the Tower of London were all utilised and by 1943 there were 1,400,000 allotments. Here Mr and Mrs Flack 'dig for victory' on Clapham Common.

Below left: Winifred Chapman shoulders her spade, ready to work on Clapham Common.

Below right: Clapham Common again - this time little Maureen Copeland helps her dad prepare the soil on their plot.

Opposite page top: It was vital for Britain to be able to produce as much food as possible. The 'Dig for Victory' campaign encouraged people to grow food in their own gardens. Here school children in Monmouthshire are growing vegetables in the school garden.

Opposite page bottom: For many women with children and with husbands in the forces it was not possible to tend an allotment. Often what was grown on the allotment or in the home garden would provide the majority of the family's fresh fruit and vegetables. Mrs Mann and Mrs Padwick and their children pictured here are visiting the allotments in Hyde Park - the produce from which was to be given to them.

CITY FARMS

Left: Tending crops within sight of the Albert Memorial in Kensington Gardens.

Below left: 'London of 1941. Park Lane, London's most expensive residential district provides us with the perfect allotment for the benefit of those "Digging for Victory". Women taking notes from the gardener who is giving hints as to the best way of producing vegetables.'

Below right: These people are tending their allotments during the Easter of 1942 in response to a call to stay at home during the holiday period so that the railway lines would be left clear for urgent war transport.

Opposite page top: Hurlingham Polo Club gave over their grounds rent-free to Fulham Borough Council for use as allotments.

Opposite page below: 'There is a prosperous farm about a quarter of an acre in extent, tucked away under the shadow of St Giles, Cripplegate, which was damaged in the 1940 air raids. Firemen from the station across the way made it, almost everything there, except the livestock, was provided by the blitz. The bricks for the pigsties came from bombed buildings, so does the wood from which the fowl-houses and the "tomatory" are made. On it there are almost every vegetable known to gardeners, and six apple trees, reputed to be the only apple trees in the City.'

Chapter Seven

A WARTIME CHILDHOOD

The war lasted for six years and for many children the war encompassed the bulk of their childhood. It was a time of danger and fear, of dislocation and loss, but it was also paradoxically a time of unprecedented freedom for many children and the community spirit engendered by the war made them feel secure. There were also many ways in which children were encouraged to, and did, contribute to the war effort.

Images of evacuation are those we most readily associate with children during the war years. The official evacuation schemes began even before war was declared and for the purposes of the system Britain was divided into three sorts of areas. Evacuation areas were those in danger of bombing; reception areas were those in country towns and villages which were considered safe and where people were expected to offer billets to those from evacuation areas; neutral areas were where no one was to leave or to evacuate to.

In the first weeks of the war nearly four million people, including pregnant women, mothers of pre-school children and disabled people, as well as children, moved from evacuation to reception areas. Evacuation schemes carried on throughout the war with peaks of the numbers evacuated directly related to the amount of bombing. After the 'phoney war' of the first year, many children returned home, only to be re-evacuated when the Blitz began. Some children who had been evacuated to the South Coast of England from the London area had to be relocated when the area suffered attacks during the summer of 1940.

Children of school age were evacuated without their parents. They were required to report to their school with only a change of clothes, basic toilet essentials, a packed lunch and, of course, a gas mask. At the school they were labelled with luggage labels, especially important for the youngest who may not have known their address. Teachers and helpers took the children on buses and trains to the reception areas. Trips as long as twelve hours were reported and many children arrived exhausted by the journey, upset at leaving their parents and fearful of what was in store for them.

For many children evacuation was the major impact of the war on their lives. The clash of cultures between the city children and their new life in the countryside was a source of problems for all concerned. Children from the poorest areas in the major cities often lived in squalid conditions with no running water. Consequently, they were often unwashed and full of minor infections like scabies and impetigo. While this horrified their host families they were generally understanding and worked hard to accept them into their homes. Sometimes the difference in standards was the other way round and children with baths and electric lights found themselves staying in farm labourers' cottages with no running water or electricity.

Some children found the countryside disturbing as they had never before experienced the quietness, the solitude or the animals, both farm animals and wildlife. Others enjoyed the space and the freedom to be able to play in the fields and lanes. Almost all, whatever their circumstances, grew to hold their host families in affection and many formed relationships which continue to this day. There was generally a determination on both sides to 'make things work' as a contribution to the war effort.

One of the most enjoyable things for children about the start of the war was the fact that it extended the school summer holidays. The government initially announced an indefinite extension but in the reception areas most schools were re-opened by the middle of September. It took slightly longer in the towns and cities as schools could only open once they had air raid shelters and then could only teach the number of pupils they had shelter space for. In effect this meant part-time schooling, with a shift system in operation - younger pupils in the morning, older ones in the afternoon. This was often the case in the countryside as well as the influx of evacuees usually meant that the village school could not accommodate all the children at once.

With so many children out of school for long periods - many with no parents at home because father was with the forces or working, and mother working as well - there was an increase in vandalism and hooliganism. Public air raid shelters were wrecked so many times by children that in the end they had to be kept locked, opened by the ARP warden when the alert sounded. However, many children just enjoyed the freedom from pressing adult scrutiny to play imaginary games and collect war 'souvenirs'. Bits of bombs and crashed planes were collected from bomb and crash sites and traded among children. This obviously unsafe activity was discouraged in varying degrees by adults.

Despite the impression given, children did not spend the war years running wild and uncontrollable around the bomb sites of Britain; they contributed a great deal

'The Lost Worshippers. This picture was taken yesterday at a church a few yards from the London school bombed in the day raid last week. A week before nearly 200 attended the service. Now the pews are empty but for a few children who survived the Luftwaffe's attack.'

Canadian soldiers at a garden party in Surrey entertained young evacuees in May 1941.

to the war effort. Children helped their parents in the 'Dig for Victory' campaign by working in their gardens or allotments. They also often joined teams 'lending a hand on the land', working on farms to boost food production. Many of the 'drives' co-ordinated by the WVS relied on children to help out. They picked wild fruits and plants such as blackberries, crab apples, mushrooms and dandelion leaves which were eaten raw, cooked or made into preserves. Children were also part of the teams collecting wild rosehips which teams of women then turned into rosehip syrup. This rich source of vitamin C was then given to children. The WVS 'salvage' drives which relied on door-to-door collection of unused household items and waste which provided some of the raw material for munitions, also relied on children's labour.

For those times that children did not want to be as active as 'playing out' or labouring for the war effort there was a limited range of activities for them. Board games, cards and reading were all popular pastimes, especially in the shelters where there was little else to occupy them. The radio was the most popular form of entertainment and there were programmes, like 'Children's Hour', broadcast specially for children. Saturday morning cinema was the other important source of entertainment specifically for children. They would watch short films and cartoons and there was always a serial such as 'Tarzan', 'The Lone Ranger' or 'Flash Gordon' which left the hero on a cliffhanger to encourage audiences back the next week.

THE EAST END EVACUATES EARLY

Left: Carrying their gas masks carefully, these East End school children leave in procession for their evacuation destinations on the day before war was declared. Although many parents had privately taken the decision to evacuate their children to safe areas - often abroad to places like Canada, the official evacuation began on the 30th August 1939.

Below: Evacuees boarding the bus at Edgware Station on 1st September 1939. Most are dressed in school clothes. Although it was still officially the summer holidays, children had to report to their school with only the belongings they could carry. The children were labelled and accompanied by their teachers.

Opposite page top: A convoy of buses on the Kingston by-pass, carrying schoolchildren to a mainline station for evacuation by train.

Opposite page bottom: Children with their belongings asleep on the floor of their classroom. They had gathered there the day before to be registered and processed, then they slept, ready for their evacuation journey the following day.

THE SECOND WAVE

Left: In December 1939 the second official evacuation scheme started. These children reading the 'Nipper' annual are part of a group leaving for Devon and Christmas in new surroundings.

Below left: These rather solemn children at Waterloo Station are part of the second wave of evacuation which relocated 10,000 children.

Below right: A somewhat more cheerful group on board the train.

Opposite page top: June 1940 and the retreat from Dunkirk prompted more mass evacuations. These children wait at Paddington Station for the train to pull out to take them to their evacuation destination.

Opposite page bottom: These evacuees are just passing through London where they are handed refreshments. Originally evacuated to the South-East they are en-route to a safe area.

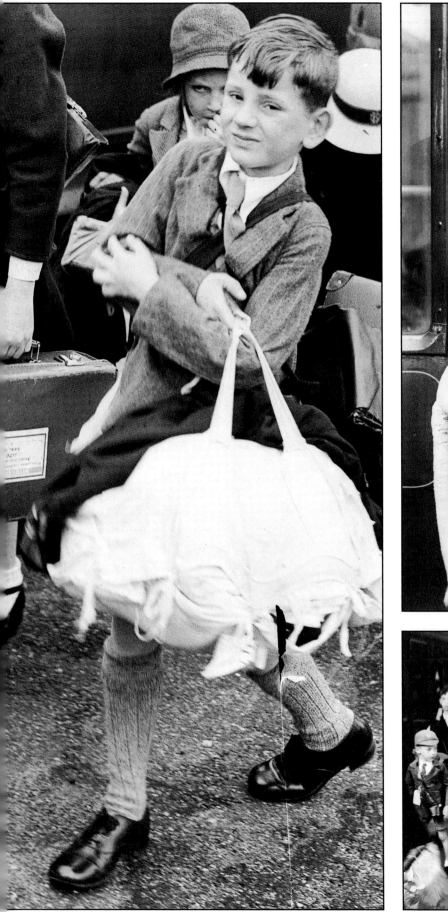

SEEKING SAFETY

Opposite page top left: Many children were initially sent to the countryside in South-East England but this area proved to be vulnerable to attack, especially during the summer of 1940 and the Battle of Britain. During that summer many children, like this young boy, who had been evacuated from London to the South-East, were transferred to the West Country.

Opposite page top right: 'The British lion took a bow at the train window yesterday when this party of schoolgirls were being evacuated from the South-East coast to the west of England.'

Opposite page below: A police escort for these children on Waterloo Station to catch a train to the West Country.

Below: In one day 10,000 children travelled from London and the Medway towns to billets in Monmouth and Glamorgan. These schoolgirls seem happy about the prospect.

Right: This young Londoner, 'labelled and loaded' gets ready to leave for safety after the continuing Blitz on London.

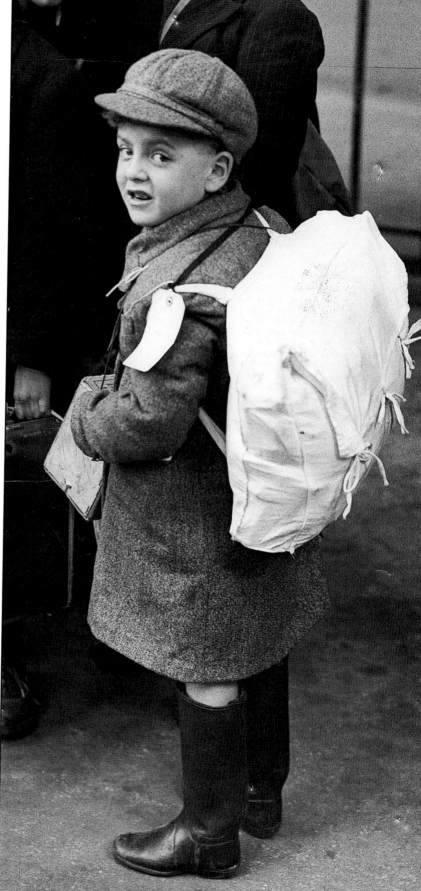

THUMBS UP!

Above: 'Thumbs up' from these youngsters. In June 1940 they were just a few of the 120,000 London children evacuated.

Left: These schoolgirls select books to read on their long journey to the country. They are the survivors from a daylight bombing raid in which their school in Catford was hit, killing twenty-three children. This large loss of young lives caused much public anguish, especially as it was January 1943 and many had thought that the threat of bombing had diminished.

Opposite page: 'After the vicious Nazi attack on London last Wednesday (16th April 1941), all arguments against the evacuation of children have been settled in those areas badly blitzed, and nine times the usual number under the LCC evacuation scheme are now leaving London. An engine driver says "hello" to evacuees at a London station.'

MODEL EVACUEES
LEAD THE WAY

Left: The King family, Allen, Roy, Doris and Lydia, were chosen as 'model' evacuees to promote evacuation schemes. They are pictured in September 1942 before they left for their new billets in the country. As the bombing of British towns and cities seemed less of a threat, increasing numbers of children returned home. There were campaigns both to discourage the return of evacuees and to encourage the evacuation of more children.

Middle left: Smiling children used to promote the benefits of evacuation. Taken after the first evacuees left their homes it was intended to reassure the parents left behind and to encourage more people in safe areas to offer billets to evacuees.

Bottom left: 'Children making their way up a hillside agleam with flowers.' A picture taken in the first week of the evacuation to show the life the children were experiencing in the reception areas.

Opposite page top left: Dulwich College boys sorting out their luggage when they were evacuated to a new school at Tonbridge in Kent.

Opposite page top right: This notice announces to parents the safe arrival of a party of school children evacuated just before the declaration of war.

Opposite page bottom: 'A day with the evacuated children in the country. East End children and others enjoying the sunshine in Berkshire, reading letters from home.'

A DIFFERENT LIFE

Opposite page top: These six children evacuated from Bow in London to Mrs Crossingham's home near Woking would have found many differences between their home life and the comforts of a middle-class bungalow.

Opposite page below: For those evacuated to the country home of Lord Blanesburgh life would have been very different. Here they are pictured listening to the evening radio broadcast of 'Children's Hour'.

Above: Evacuated from a Dr Barnardo's Home in Middlesbrough to Ripley Castle these girls probably found a big difference in surroundings, but perhaps not much difference to their way of life.

Middle right: These youngsters being read to by a nurse are evacuees from the Channel Islands which were occupied by German troops at the end of June 1940. A decision had been taken that the islands could not be defended and in the weeks prior to the invasion many people were evacuated, along with livestock and crops. However, many others had to live until August 1944 under German occupation.

Bottom right: This looks rather austere and unwelcoming - the boys' washroom at a camp near Farnham. While every effort was made to billet evacuees in homes, it was sometimes necessary for groups of schoolchildren to be billeted in camps.

LEARNING NEW SKILLS

Left: Two evacuees, Robert Yoghill and William Williams from Islington, London are shown how to milk the cows by Miss Eileen Hocking on her family farm in Cornwall.

Top: 'A raid on the village shop. The youngsters who have been evacuated from London to this Berkshire village, soon found the position of the local "sweets and toys" shop. Here are some of them doing a little window gazing before shopping.' This picture was taken in October 1940 when it was still possible to buy sweets off the ration.

Above: 'London kiddies evacuated to a little Welsh village are attending the village school. One of the most important lessons is the Welsh language instruction, for many of the villagers know no English.'

BEACH INVASION!

Above: These evacuated city children paddle in the sea on the second day of the war. This freedom to spend time on the beaches was short-lived.

Left: Soon the beaches around Britain's shores were mined and covered with barbed wire. These boys can only gaze longingly at the sea.

Opposite page: Four energetic evacuees off for a dip.

TOGETHER AGAIN

Opposite page top left: Mrs Elliott of Tottenham runs to greet her six daughters in October 1939. It was the first time they had been together since the girls were evacuated to Saffron Walden in September.

Opposite page top right: A hug for the youngest.

Opposite page bottom left: All together again.

Opposite page bottom right: A young girl searches her father's pockets for a treat in their first meeting for almost two months.

Left: September 1944 and these tired and weary travellers at Euston are returning evacuees. Much of the return was rather piecemeal - families collected their evacuated children, rather than the mass movement there had been when they left.

Below: The Good family returned to London after a 5-year-long absence to find it much changed. Some families could not bear to be separated and so moved all together to areas of safety. Many families did not, or could not, return to their original homes but made a new life for themselves in the area they had evacuated to.

SCHOOL RETURNS

Children who remained in areas likely to be bombed had to be protected. Each school had its own air raid shelter facilities. Here at Mayville Road School in Leyton the headmistress shows the infants the sandbagged trenches to shelter them in the event of a raid.

Opposite page top: 'Back to school - with their gas masks.' Like many schools, Grange Park School, North London, had not re-opened at the beginning of September, but did so on 20th September. The children were not compelled to attend but most did, bringing their gas masks with them.

Opposite page bottom: Kennington Road Girls' School pictured at the end of the war. It had been blitzed in 1940 and hit by a flying bomb in 1944 but lessons continued in the draughty classrooms.

LESSONS OF THE WAR

Top left: 'The "lesson" the children enjoy. Air raid practice drill has now become the most popular activity, at the Wood End Infants School, Ealing. The trenches, which are among the best-equipped in Middlesex schools, can take five hundred children. They have comfortable seats and their own Red Cross Unit.'

Top right: Reading comics and singing 'Ten Green Bottles', these children and their teachers take cover in the school shelter during an air raid alarm on the South-East coast.

Left: Boys of Eton School find the place changed when they returned from their summer vacation in 1939. Here three boys, carrying gas masks, examine the sandbagged entrance to an air raid shelter.

Opposite page top: 'The mighty atom - the national savings campaign in schools.' Children were encouraged, like their parents, to contribute to the war effort by putting their money into National Savings. Teachers were asked to help by organising collections, as here in a Kent school.

Opposite page bottom: 'Boys of the Workington and Cumberland Technical and Secondary School who are in their final year help in the making of munitions by staying behind and working after school hours.'

DIG FOR VICTORY

Left: Etonians on 'Long Leave' spent their time working on allotments normally tended by members of the Eton Working Men's Allotment Society.

Below: London children helping out with the hop picking joined in an open-air service on a National Day of Prayer in September 1941.

Opposite page top: 'The heart of Britain. In the spirit of this picture, in blitzed Bristol, fair and historic city. In Bristol they have danced the May Dances, always, and amid the wrecked homes the children still dance the May-days, and their elders still watch them.'

Opposite page below left: Schoolboys in Essex examine incendiary bombs which fell in their school grounds. There was a great fascination for children, especially boys, in collecting war 'souvenirs' - no doubt this incendiary would become part of someone's collection.

Opposite page below right: A Harrow School boy with some of his 'souvenirs', collected from the school grounds after raids during the Blitz. The boys traded the souvenirs among themselves for money which was donated to the 'Spitfire Fund'.

TIME FOR TEA

Four boys take tea in the garden of their damaged home after a daylight raid in March 1943.

Opposite page top left: Children from a London orphanage survey the wreckage of their home after it was hit during the Blitz.

Opposite page top right: Coventry schoolboys after a particularly heavy raid in April 1941, are fed in the street by a mobile canteen donated by the Americans.

Opposite page bottom: The child at play on the home-made cart calmly reads the danger notice.

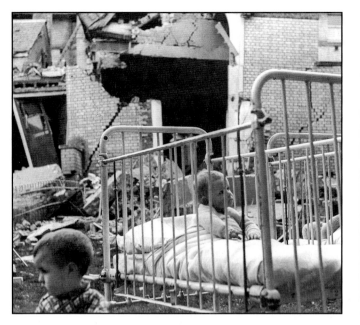

CHILDREN'S PROBLEMS

Above: 'Watch your gas mask. Wendy brings her gas mask to be repaired. The rubber is perished and has small holes in the face piece.'

Left: This little girl, Pat, was having her first gas mask fitted, comforted by her mother. She would have previously been put in a respirator suit which covered the whole of an infant's body.

Opposite page top and bottom: In March 1941 there were concerns by the Council in Dover about the increase in the child population. This was probably a response to the increasing number of children left unsupervised for quite long periods of time rather than a significant increase in numbers. With the number of hours their parents were required to work or spend in ensuring the necessities of life were covered, many children were often left to their own devices.

Chapter Eight

KEEP SMILING THROUGH

Despite the danger and the death, the rationing and shortages, the Blackout and dislocation, the hard work to keep life as normal as possible and the endless labour for the war effort, there was a tremendous spirit in the British population. That spirit manifested itself in the dogged determination to carry on whatever the dangers, the sense of community and most noticeably the good humour with which life was generally conducted. In the words of Vera Lynn's song the majority of the population did 'keep smiling through', often with comic good humour.

The government worked sensitively to promote the idea of working together to defeat an enemy which needed to be stopped. Unlike the propaganda of the First World War which focussed on the evilness of the Germans, or 'the Hun', most propaganda campaigns of the Second World War emphasised social responsibility - 'Careless talk costs lives', 'Dig for victory', 'Women, join the factories', 'Do not waste food'. Salvage drives in which people donated household items such as pots and pans encouraged the feeling of contributing directly to the war effort. A more subtle sort of propaganda took place in films and documentaries shown in cinemas - attractive and glamorous young men and women in factories, army camps, airbases or on ships all working together to protect the British way of life which was under threat from Hitler.

Public morale was also closely monitored and any contentious issues were thought through carefully. When people first started sheltering in the Underground there was government resistance as they were anxious to avoid a 'deep shelter mentality' in which citizens spent all their time underground. Under pressure from the public, and when this proved not to be the case, the government conceded. Government were also careful to keep in place morale-boosting production such as that of cosmetics and chocolate, and did not turn every factory over to the wholesale production of munitions. There were also extra rations at special times like Christmas.

Another way in which the government helped to promote the idea of a community spirit was through the rationing system which provided fair shares for all. It did not matter how rich you were, everyone got the same official ration. Prices of rationed and unrationed goods were strictly controlled to avoid profiteering. Although the rich could buy some more expensive, specially tailored clothing, it was generally not possible to buy something no one else could afford, unless it was purchased on the 'black market'. Even the Royal Family rationed themselves and stuck to the five-inch-deep bath once a week, recommended to save fuel.

Everyone rose to the challenges of rationing and shortages. Creative ideas for cake recipes without eggs, fats, sugar; recipes to make meat and fish go further; recipes using food gathered from the wild; recipes for substitute foodstuffs, such as banana-flavoured parsnip as a sandwich filling, were shared by women. Everyone worked hard to 'make do and mend'; children would be involved in unravelling old wool for re-use; men would mend old shoes and make toys and games for children; women would patch, sew and repair torn and old clothing. Most people, while often depressed by the shortages, took pride in their ingenuity and skill.

There was also tremendous pride in 'business as usual' - a legend which could be seen all over, most especially after a bombing raid. And yet while every-one carried on as usual, there was an understanding that much had changed. Women formed a huge percentage of the workforce, gone were the pre-war bans on married women working. There was a breaking down of the class barriers as people mixed through evacuation, in shelters and in the workplace. With the publication in 1944 of plans for free secondary education and a National Health Service,

'Methodically the German airmen hit hospitals whenever they manage to penetrate the London barrage, and when a bomb fell on this hospital last night a nurse was killed. Nevertheless, her comrades went immediately to work when daylight came to clear up.'

the aim was to provide access to good health and education provision for all.

One important area for keeping up spirits was entertainment. As soon as war broke out all places of public entertainment, such as cinemas, theatres, concert halls and football grounds were closed down to avoid the possibility of many people being killed in a direct hit on a crowded area. When no bombing came many venues re-opened with air raid precautions in place.

However, the football programme, like many other sports, was severely curtailed, as many professional footballers were drafted into the army. Players in the forces could play as guest players for any club they chose if they were on leave from their unit, but most teams were made up of teenage boys. The leagues were re-organised into areas so that clubs did not

'The road to business was not easy. But the girls picked their way through the debris with a laugh and a smile - the spirit of the City after "reprisals". This picture was taken after the 10th May 1941 raid which was the last major, and most devastating, raid of the Blitz on London.

have to travel long distances for games. By 1943 football was almost as well attended as it had been before the war.

While many theatres re-opened in 1939, not all did so - some closed for the duration. Again, this was largely due to lack of personnel. Many actors were called up and there were not the actors to sustain a full programme in the West End for example. Many provincial and seaside theatres also closed. Some theatres and concert halls changed function - the Drury Lane Theatre was taken over by the forces' entertainment unit, ENSA, and the Royal Opera House was used as a dance hall.

Cinema proved to be one of the most important forms of public entertainment. Many of the Hollywood movies such as 'Gone With the Wind' drew huge audiences. There was also a British film industry which continued throughout the war. Its output ranged from Noel Coward's 'In Which We Serve' and Laurence Olivier's 'Henry V' to 'Desert Victory', a documentary shot by Roy Boulting during the battle for El Alamein, and a host of public information films and newsreels.

The BBC were proud of the fact that they never failed to transmit their programming throughout the war. There were no other broadcasters at this time and with the outbreak of war the BBC cut out their embryonic television channel and all their radio stations bar one. This one station was very important for morale during the war. Not only did the public feel they were getting a fair news picture, the BBC also broadcast programmes which became national institutions. Popular programmes included 'The Brains Trust', 'Woman's Hour', 'Children's Hour', 'Forces' Favourites', and 'Music While You Work'. But the most popular programme was ITMA (It's That Man Again), starring Tommy Handley - the programme consisted of sketches which made fun of everyone involved in the war, epitomising the spirit and humour of the nation.

HITLER'S BOMBS CAN'T BEAT US

Above: This photograph captures many of the facets of Britain during the war - the bomb damage, the shelter signs, the poster urging donations to the 'Spitfire Fund', the community spirit of the residents chatting on a street corner, and the spirit of defiance, the urge to 'Keep - Smiling'.

Left: This boot repair shop in Battersea signals it is closed for the duration after its proprietor was called up in the first week of the war.

Opposite page: Serving among the bombed ruins of a London street at the height of the Blitz, this street fruit seller not only has oranges, which he proudly boasts have come through the Mediterranean, Musso's (Mussolini's) 'Lake', but also has bananas for sale.

WE CAN TAKE IT AND LAUGH

Opposite page top left: 'I can take it and laugh. Humour seems to creep through everywhere. An amusing offer seen in London after a bomb had demolished a dwelling house.'

Opposite page top right: Pictured towards the end of the Blitz this photograph demonstates that the bombing had not demoralised the British people; there was no pressure on the government to seek peace, which was the intention of the German bombing campaign.

Opposite page bottom: 'British humour prevails through weeks of air raids: a comic police notice. Many street notices in London testify to the fact that in spite of the air raids British people are smiling through with characteristic humour. Here is a policeman's effort in the London area, warning passers-by to pass by quickly in a danger zone.'

Right: An ironic message for the milkman from the residents of this Hackney street.

Below: This ARP shelter demonstrates the fighting spirit of Britain in its humorously excessive way.

BUSINESS AS USUAL

Hanging out the Union Jacks and declaring that they are still open for business in this bombed-out shop in south-west London.

Opposite page top: A hairdresser's in the West End of London after a raid. The legend 'Business as Usual' and the Union Jack were two of the most frequently seen symbols of British morale.

Opposite page below: Taken in May 1941 after what was in effect the final and worst raid on London in the period of concentrated bombing called 'the Blitz', this messenger puzzles out where to redirect his packages - the details of the companies' new addresses are hung on a string across the road leading to the bombed-out street which once housed them.

DANCE PARTNERS

Opposite page top left: An open-air dance at Brockwell Park in London in the summer of 1941. With the majority of young men in the forces the young women partner each other.

Opposite page bottom left: Chelsea pensioners washing crockery salvaged from the Royal Hospital after it was damaged during a raid in November 1940.

Opposite page right: A queue for a special service at St Martin's Church. The Church played a significant role in the war, organising National Days of Prayer and special services to cater for the country's spiritual needs, but also helping out practically and socially through its various charitable organisations.

Left: Sign in Lambeth Walk which was closed to traffic but open for business after an attack early in the Blitz.

Below: Shoppers and stall holders carrying on 'business as usual' after a raid on Lambeth Walk during September 1940.

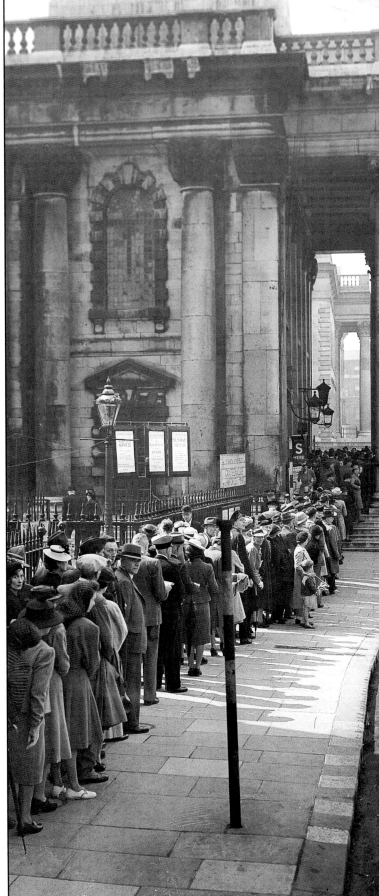

LIFE GOES ON

Above: 'Pictured in Charing Cross, a Canadian soldier gives a girl a buttonhole of spring primroses.'

Left: 'Foyle's opened a library in a former refreshment kiosk in Hyde Park. Here, on its opening day, Miss Christina Foyle and a group of overseas troops examine some of the books available to borrow. It was difficult to obtain paper for new books so libraries were very popular.

Opposite page top left: 'To overcome the telephonic and telegraphic difficulties in the City of London the Post Office today (11th January 1941) instituted a street telegram service. Messengers wearing appropriate notices parade in the streets within the vicinity of Northgate House and Regina House ready to receive telegrams.'

Opposite page top right: The 'Mobile Post Office' provides a 'desk' for this customer while also transacting payment.

Opposite page bottom left: 'A newspaper seller in Fleet Street said people still wanted newspapers during the warnings and has supplied a tin hat for himself and stops at his post. His tin hat seems to give him security.'

Opposite page bottom right: The gas man carries on with his tin helmet, attending to damaged gas mains.

FEEDING THE NATION

Opposite page top: A photograph of a London street market during the first weeks of the war taken to promote the idea that there was no shortage of food, to try to prevent panic buying and real shortages occurring.

Opposite page bottom left: These people are queuing for a 'British Restaurant', a system of restaurants where for 1s 2d (6p) it was possible to buy a good quality three course meal. It was not necessary to use ration coupons for these meals and so they provided a valuable addition to the ration, as well as saving their customers valuable time by cooking their main meal of the day.

Opposite page bottom right: Customers admire the menu at a British Restaurant. This particular London restaurant, serving 500 lunches daily, was to extend its opening hours to serve hot meals to those, like firewatchers and ARP wardens, on duty at night.

Above: A war factory canteen. As the war progressed facilities for workers improved to include, in the larger factories, canteens serving hot food over and above the ration.

Left: Refreshments were also provided in the shelters, in some of the larger ones there were canteens serving hot meals. Here 72-year old Mrs Ramsey receives her 3501st cup of tea in Holborn Tube station where she had frequently sheltered from air raids.

EAT MORE POTATOES

Above: Lord Woolton, the Minister of Food, headed many campaigns to encourage the avoidance of food waste and to encourage the eating of unusual or plentiful foods. These baked potatoes are on sale at Paddington Station as an experiment to support the 'Eat More Potatoes' campaign.

Right: Servicemen buy roast potatoes from a street seller in a port in the North of England. Potatoes were not rationed and provided a filling meal.

Opposite page top: These men and women are volunteers who, working with the Ministry of Food, served more than 12,000 meals to the people of Dover who sheltered in these caves during the periods of the most intense shelling from the French coast.

Opposite page bottom: Being fed in a communal centre on the coast of North-East England, these people were bombed out of their homes. They stayed at the centre until their houses could be repaired or new accommodation found for them.

DON'T PANIC!

Knitting comfortably in Trafalgar Square as the air raid siren wails.

Opposite page top: Londoners sit on the steps of St Martin-in-the-Fields during an air raid warning in the last days of August 1940. At this point in the war the bombing was not as intense as it was to become just two weeks later, so they could risk sitting calmly in the sunshine.

Opposite page bottom: 'Why don't you take cover?' 'We always drive them away.' 'It's too warm to take shelter today,' were the replies.

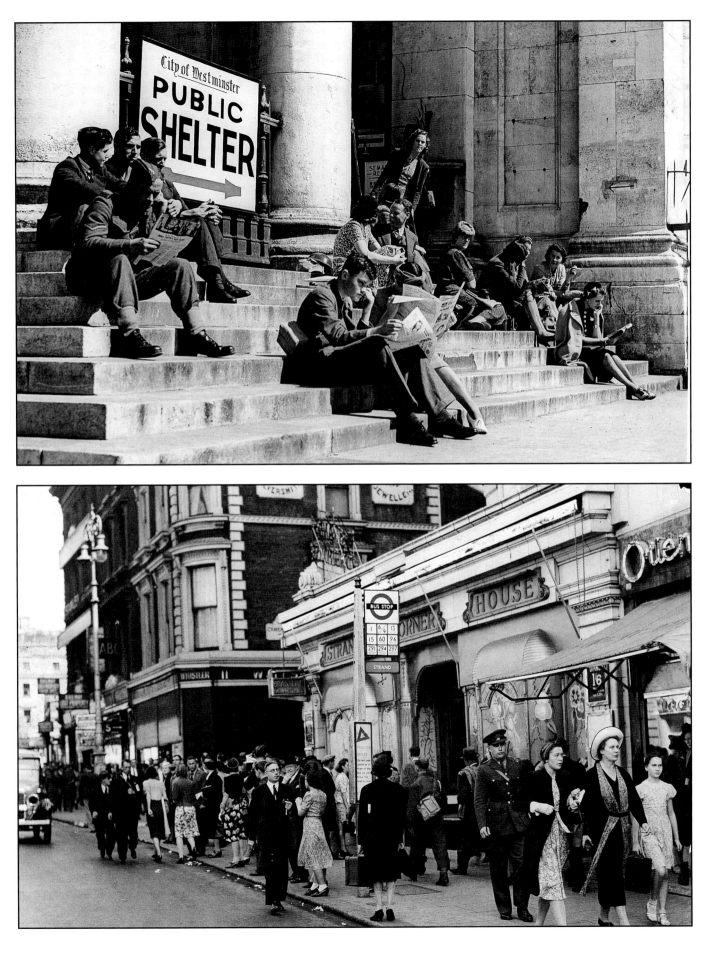

'CARRY-ON' CITY

Left top and middle: On Monday 30th December, 1940, the morning after the raid that caused the second Fire of London, workers walk to work past the fire tenders and burnt-out buildings.

Below: 'Outside their fire-wrecked office the staff of a City firm queue up to draw their weekly pay. A small table was the cashier's "office". On the ground lay a blackened typewriter - yesterday's glimpse of the "carry-on" City.'

Opposite page top: Soldiers help City clerks to salvage books after the Fire Blitz on Sunday 29th December, 1940. Workers would have to spend time painstakingly checking and reconstituting records.

Opposite page bottom left: The Lord Mayor of London inspecting books salvaged from the Guildhall Library.

Opposite page bottom right: Temporary reconstruction of the Guildhall roof to enable the building to be used again. The medieval building lost its roof in the fire, although the ancient walls remained relatively intact. All over Britain people worked tirelessly to make buildings safe. Sometimes demolition was the only option but where it could be repaired, even temporarily, the work was done.

CHANGING SCENES

Left: A Military Policeman takes over traffic duty in Whitehall, part of the increasing appearance of uniforms on the streets of Britain in the early weeks of the war.

Below left: Painting London Tube signs with ultra-violet paint so that they could be read more easily in the Blackout. The Blackout changed the night-time landscape of Britain's towns and cities. It was the one thing that the majority of people said they found most inconvenient about the war.

Below right: Illuminating the sign with ultra-violet light, which would not seem that different to the bluish blackout lights.

GETTING AWAY FROM IT ALL

Top: August Bank Holiday 1941, and despite the government's plea to 'stay at home' Paddington Station, as a result of petrol rationing, has more travellers than it could have expected before the war.

Middle: This woman was determined to make the most of her day at the seaside on August Bank Holiday, 1944. By this time there was virtually no threat of an invasion and gradually the bans on access to the beaches were lifted.

Bottom: But not at Angmering where this is the closest these mothers and children can get to the sea, although almost 2,000 yards of the beach had been cleared for access by the military.

NEW WAYS OF GETTING TO WORK

Opposite page top: The Ministry of Transport instituted a new river boat service between Westminster and Woolwich. Petrol rationing meant the more public transport could be used the greater the saving and the more smoothly the capital would run.

Opposite page bottom: Travellers could buy tickets on board the river boat service but people with 'tickets for the relative land journeys may use them'. The river boat service helped remove road congestion caused by Blitz debris and eased the strain on the bomb-damaged bus stock.

Above: 'Sunday workers, answering the call for 7-day-a-week output effort, were to be seen in many parts of England hurrying to and from their jobs today (26th May 1940). This picture was taken in a northern suburb of London.'

Left: City office workers hitch a lift with motorists who do have petrol for their cars.

ON THE BUSES

Left: In October 1940, during the Blitz, London bus drivers and conductors were issued with tin helmets in recognition of the fact that they were frequently in danger when the bombing started.

Below left: Buses were brought in from the Provinces to supplement London buses and to replace those lost during the Blitz. This Manchester Corporation bus is pictured in the process of having its destination roll changed.

Below right: A bus brought in from the Provinces on duty in Fleet Street.

Opposite page: When all else fails - go to work on a horse. Horse-drawn traffic, which by the start of the war was becoming a rarity on the streets of London, dramatically increased in number. Horses, while needing food for fuel, provided a neat solution to the problem of petrol rationing when it came to delivering bulky or heavy loads.

BUS STRIKE

Opposite page top: In April 1944 London bus drivers went on strike. The government responded by bringing the army in. Here women workers wait patiently for the emergency service.

Opposite page bottom: Boarding an army lorry at Hackney during the bus strike.

Left: 'This one's full. The next one will be along in a minute.'

Below left: Soldiers also drove the buses. Here a London transport instructor gives directions to an army driver before he takes his bus out on the road.

Below right: 'Pulling out into the traffic in Park Lane.'

HOPE AND PRAYER

On the fourth anniversary of the outbreak of war a National Day of Prayer was organised. This picture was taken at 11.00 a.m. in Trafalgar Square.

Below: Again in Trafalgar Square, a meeting to hear speakers from all political parties express their views on the importance of victory in that year, 1942.

CONCERT PARTY

Above: A concert at the Royal Albert Hall for the
Home Guard, sponsored by the Daily Mail.

Left: A close-up of the crowd at the Home Guard
concert. Entertainment was extremely important for
keeping up morale. In the first weeks of the war all
cinemas and theatres closed down. Not all theatres
reopened but many cinemas did and together with the
radio were the mainstay of the majority of people's
entertainment. Live entertainment like this concert
was rarer and much appreciated.

Below: A Home Guard unit leaving a London cinema.

Chapter Nine

VICTORY!

For the first two years the 'world' war was fought largely in Europe, although many troops from Britain's colonies were involved in the fighting. On 10th June 1940, Italy, Germany's ally declared war on Britain as part of its campaign to occupy North Africa. All of the northern shore of the Mediterranean was controlled by the Axis Powers, allies of Germany and Italy, either through occupation or threats of occupation - Spain, having just fought a bloody civil war, was neutral. If the Axis had gained control of the Mediterranean, the interests of Britain and its allies, like the Free French, would have been seriously compromised, as would British-controlled areas such as Malta and Gibraltar. So by the summer of 1940 fighting had spread to North Africa, involving the Eighth Army, the 'Desert Rats', many of whom were soldiers from British colonies.

In June 1941 Hitler launched 'Operation Barbarossa', an attack on Stalin's USSR with whom he had signed a non-aggression pact in August 1939. Immediately, the USSR became one of Britain's allies and Churchill pledged British support to the Russians. Fighting in Russia was not the blitzkrieg that had worked elsewhere in Europe; the German Army found progress slow, thousands died in sieges of major Russian towns like Stalingrad (now Volgograd) and Leningrad (now St Petersburg), and as the bitter Russian winter set in the battles were conducted in terrible conditions.

Throughout the first years while Britain had stood largely alone, the USA had given a good deal of moral and practical support in the form of food and weapons. The Lend-Lease Agreement allowed Britain to have weapons and equipment without having to pay for them immediately - they were lent for the duration of the war, to be paid for after the war was won. President Roosevelt was sympathetic but there was no real appetite for committing American troops to the fighting. When the Japanese attacked the American naval base at Pearl Harbor in Hawaii on 7th December 1941, another theatre of war was opened in the Pacific.

As 1942 opened the conflict had engulfed much of the world. There was conflict in the Pacific, Russia, North Africa, as well as Europe where it had all started. The two sides were clearly drawn - the Allies: Britain, its colonies and those remnants of European countries that had managed to escape occupied Europe, the USSR and the USA; against them were the Axis Powers: Germany, Italy and Japan. Victory was to be a slow and staggered process.

The first victory came with the surrender of Italy on 8th September 1943. This had been made possible by the victory of General Montgomery's Eighth Army at El Alamein in North Africa. On Sunday 15th November 1942 church bells rang throughout Britain for the first time since the beginning of the war. The ringing of church bells was supposed to signal an invasion but on this occasion they were ringing in celebration of the Allied victory at El Alamein. The Eighth Army fought on and in May 1943 110,000

A Soho bar where French patriots and the British celebrate the fall of Paris. Despite the celebrations in London and the progress of the Allies in France, London and the South-East had become prey to the pilotless bombs - the V1 flying bombs, nicknamed buzzbombs or doodlebugs, and the V2 rocket bombs.

German soldiers and 40,000 Italian soldiers surrendered bringing an end to the North African campaign. This victory secured a base from which to mount an assault on Italy, firstly taking the islands of Lampedusa, Pantelleria and Sicily before landing on the mainland and forcing the fall of Mussolini and the country's surrender.

1944 was a key year in the battle for an Allied victory. Russia's Red Army began to gain the upper hand against Hitler's troops, pushing them westward towards Germany. In January, the Americans landed troops at Anzio to attack the German troops which occupied Northern Italy, despite the Rome government's surrender to the Allies. And of course in June 1944, the Allies landed on the beaches of Normandy to begin to push back the Germans into Germany. Later in the year, in October, General MacArthur, leading a force of quarter of a million men, re-took the Philippines as the beginning of an all-out assault on the Japanese in the Pacific.

Throughout 1944 and early 1945, the Germans were squeezed back on several fronts - from France in the west, from Russia in the east and Italy and Greece in the south. German towns and cities were subject to some of the most devastating air raids of the war, destroying weapons production and infrastructure, and killing thousands. Despite last-ditch efforts in the Battle of the Bulge in the Ardennes and the attempts to attack Britain with the new pilotless bombs, the V1s and V2s, Germany could not hold out. On 30th April 1945, Hitler committed suicide in the face of defeat as the Red Army took control in the ruined streets of Berlin. Field Marshal Keitel signed Germany's unconditional surrender on 8th May and the victory and peace in Europe was secure.

The peace began officially at one minute past midnight on 9th May 1945 but the celebrations started during Tuesday the eighth and lasted throughout the night. While the entire country celebrated in the streets, London was the focus of the biggest festivities. All morning on the eighth, crowds had gathered in Whitehall, waiting for an official announcement of peace in Europe. An announcement was expected at 9.00 a.m. but it was not until 3.00 p.m. that Prime Minister Churchill broadcast to the nation, the news relayed through loudspeakers in the centre of London. He said that the war in Europe would end at midnight, praised the British people and their allies, while also reminding them that Japan was not yet defeated.

Churchill's broadcast was the signal for the party to begin up and down the land. An estimated 50,000 people thronged the streets of central London, many making their way to Buckingham Palace to call for the King and Queen who, together with their daughters, the Princesses Elizabeth and Margaret, and Winston Churchill, made a total of eight appearances on the royal balcony. As night fell the party continued in the streets, the licensing laws suspended for the night. Despite the fact that the war in the Pacific continued, it was a celebration of unrestrained joy after more than five and a half years of war with its dangers, deprivations and losses. On the following Sunday, prayers were said in churches throughout Britain; many were so full that services had to be relayed to those outside.

VE Day was a joyous outpouring of emotion but everyone was aware that it was not the end of the war. In Britain there were many families with members involved in action in the Pacific. The final end to the war was not to come for another three months and the surrender of the Japanese came only after the dropping of two atomic bombs, one on the city of Hiroshima on 6th August 1945; the second three days later destroyed Japan's shipbuilding centre of Nagasaki. Following days of negotiation Japan surrendered on 14th August 1945, marking the end of the Second World War. For the population of Britain the war had lasted just twenty days short of six years.

The news of the Japanese surrender was broadcast in Britain by Prime Minister Clement Attlee at midnight on the fourteenth while most of the population were sleeping. They were wakened from their beds by the sounds of ships' sirens and train whistles. Gradually people rose and congregated in streets throughout Britain, lighting bonfires specially prepared for the moment, setting off flares and fireworks. By 3.00 a.m. the crowds in Piccadilly were as large as those on VE Day. The 15th and 16th August were designated V Day public holidays; the nation celebrated and offered prayers of thanksgiving for two days before they turned to face the peace.

Fifty-five million people throughout the world had lost their lives in the conflict and for much of Europe the long process of reconstruction began. The cost of the war meant that Britain faced years of austerity. Rationing continued for a further nine years, indeed in some instances became more severe - bread, never rationed during the war, was rationed in peacetime. The nation had to turn its economy and industry from everything for the war effort to peacetime production. Millions of men and women had to be demobilised from the Armed Forces; families and communities had to learn to live together again in peacetime social structures which in many ways would be different from those in existence before 3rd September 1939.

Not only did people need to 'get back to normal' but the landscape also needed to return to what it was before the war. There were innumerable bomb sites which would remain derelict for many years. But here Eros emerges from the protective covering erected in the first weeks of the war.

ITALY SURRENDERS

Opposite page top: 'City workers reading the first news of the unconditional surrender of Italy, chalked by an enterprising news vendor on his board.' On 8th September 1943, Italy surrendered to the Allies after a lightning strike, firstly on Sicily and then on the Italian mainland.

Opposite page bottom: People in the West End of London reading the news of Italy's capitulation. Mussolini, the Fascist dictator in Italy, had been deposed soon after the Allies landed in Sicily in July 1943. He was replaced by the anti-Fascist Marshal Badoglio and the surrender soon followed.

Above: Queuing in the street for newspapers with details of the Allied invasion of mainland Europe on 6th June 1944. Almost four years to the day since the retreat from the beaches at Dunkirk British troops, together with the Allies, landed on the beaches in Normandy.

Left: Exiled French in Soho hang out the Tricolor in celebration of the fall of Paris on 24th August 1944. Their leader General de Gaulle entered the capital the next day. After fierce battles in Normandy, the Allies moved swiftly through France to recapture Paris.

THE END IS IN SIGHT

Opposite page: September 1944 and this street seller in Oxford Street senses victory. His barrow is loaded with Union Jacks of all sizes.

Above: This picture is dated 2nd May 1945 and there is conviction that the proclamation of the Allied victory in Europe is a certainty.

Right: Getting ready for the time when the lights return to normal, these workmen are replacing the globes on the street lights in Piccadilly.

Below: May 7th 1945 and crowds gather outside Downing Street and into Whitehall awaiting news of Germany's final surrender. Following Hitler's suicide on 30th April, German troops had surrendered on all fronts. All that was needed was the final signature on a declaration of unconditional surrender.

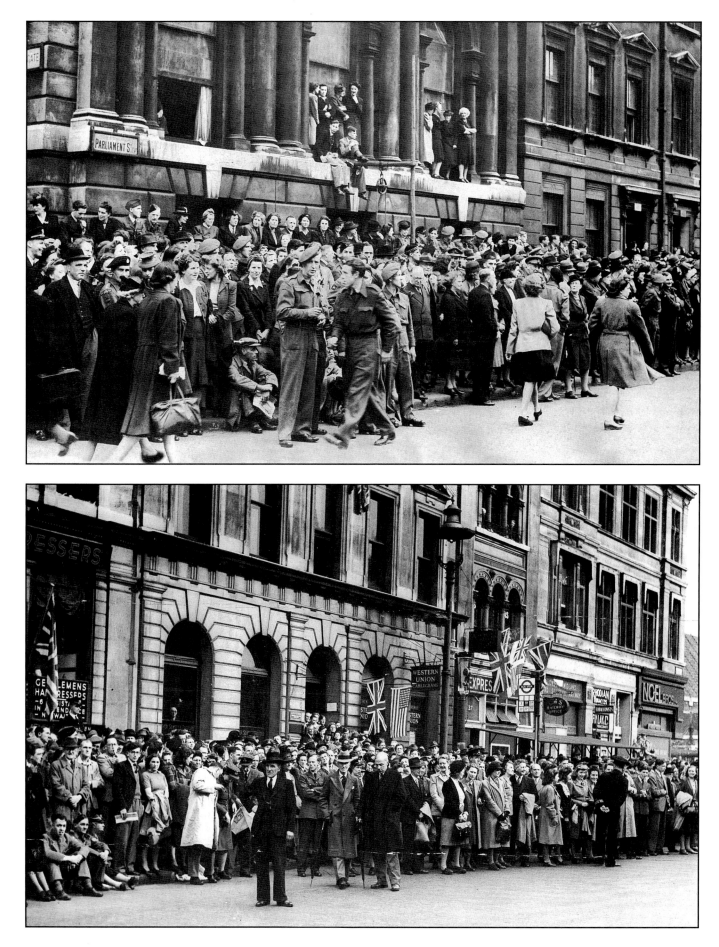

WAITING

Opposite page top: Crowds gather in Parliament Street on the 8th May, waiting for an announcement from the Prime Minister Winston Churchill from the balcony of the Ministry of Health, so the VE Day celebrations could commence.

Opposite page bottom: Waiting in the sunshine in Whitehall for the official announcement that 'This is VE Day'.

Above: Piccadilly Circus thronged with crowds meeting to hear the news they have waited over five and a half years for - the surrender of Nazi Germany.

Left: Allied forces from all the services and from all the Allied nations joined in the celebrations. Here the Australian flag flies as the crowd gathers momentum.

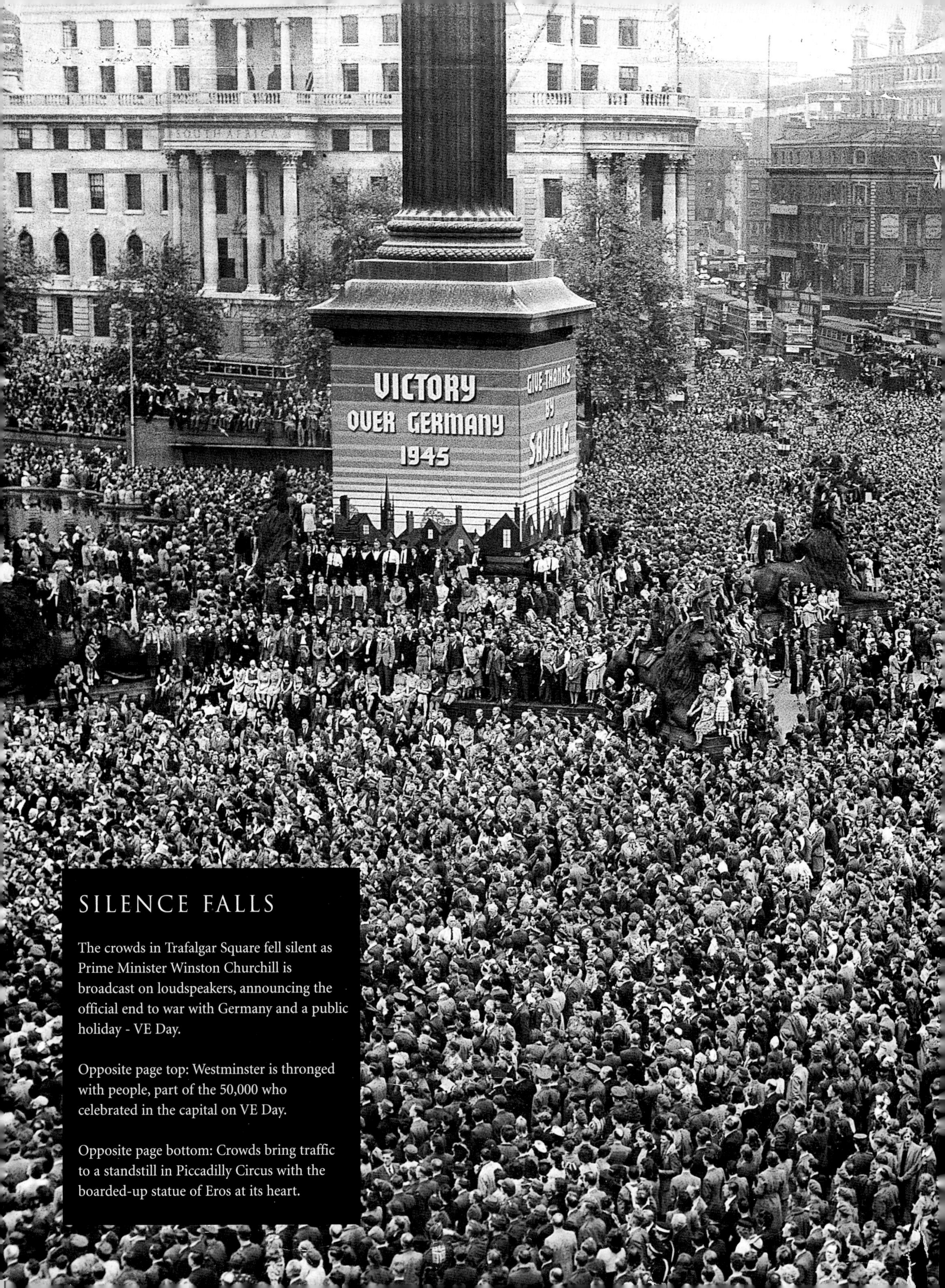

VICTORY
OVER GERMANY
1945

GIVE THANKS BY SAVING

SILENCE FALLS

The crowds in Trafalgar Square fell silent as Prime Minister Winston Churchill is broadcast on loudspeakers, announcing the official end to war with Germany and a public holiday - VE Day.

Opposite page top: Westminster is thronged with people, part of the 50,000 who celebrated in the capital on VE Day.

Opposite page bottom: Crowds bring traffic to a standstill in Piccadilly Circus with the boarded-up statue of Eros at its heart.

ON TOP OF THE WORLD

Opposite page: The more adventurous of the revellers climb Eros's protective shell.

Left: ATS and American soldiers cheer from one of the plinths in Trafalgar Square.

Below: Fortunately it was a warm sunny day, as befitted the mood of the nation, but these women and sailors probably wouldn't have cared whatever the weather as they paddle in the Trafalgar Square fountains!

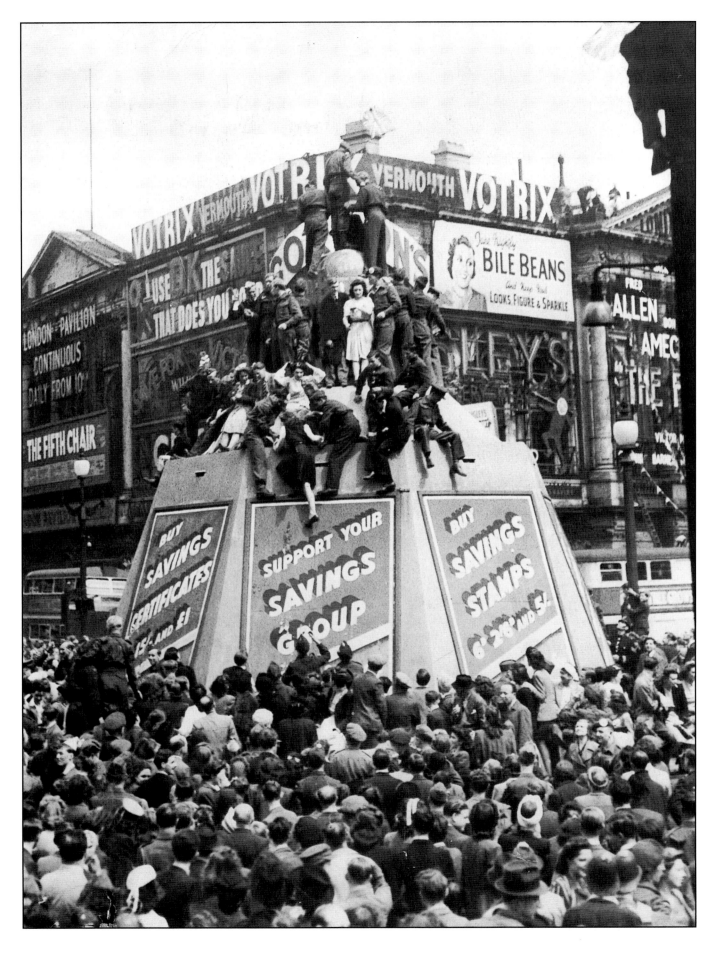

WE WANT THE KING!

Opposite page top: Gathering outside Buckingham Palace on VE Day. The Royal Family had remained in the Palace for the duration of the war, shunning the idea of evacuation to a safer area, a gesture that was much appreciated by the nation.

Opposite page bottom: The crowd wait and call for the King to appear on the Palace balcony.

Left: A cheer goes up for the King, Queen and the Princesses Elizabeth and Margaret as they appear on the balcony. Later Prime Minister Churchill joined them.

Below: The King and Queen wave to the crowds while Churchill and the two Princesses smile. Later on in the evening, Princess Elizabeth and Princess Margaret left the Palace to join the revellers in the streets.

THE NATION'S LEADERS

Opposite page: The King and Winston Churchill photographed together in the grounds of Buckingham Palace.

Above: Churchill, members of the Cabinet and the Chiefs of Staff with the King at Buckingham Palace which became the centre for much of the celebrations during the daylight hours.

Left: Mounted policemen hold back the crowds as Winston Churchill, with other members of the Houses of Parliament walked to St Margaret's church for a service of thanksgiving on VE Day.

A BRILLIANT NIGHT

Floodlights illuminate the cross on top of St Paul's Cathedral.

Right: Admiralty Arch floodlit on the night of VE Day. After the focus on the Palace during the day, the crowd moved down the Mall to join others in Piccadilly where licensing laws had been suspended for the night.

V FOR VICTORY

The flags are hung out, the victory sign chalked on the cobbles and the residents of this street in Hunslet, Leeds, gather to celebrate.

Opposite page top left: A children's party organised by residents of Kentwell Close in Brockley, South London, to celebrate VE Day.

Opposite page bottom left: 'Street tea parties celebrate "V" Whitsun. Not everybody went from London to the seaside and other places this Whitsun (21st May 1945). Some preferred to stay at home like these residents of Tilloch Street, Islington, who organised tea parties in the street for the children, complete with paper hats and decorations.'

THANKSGIVING

Above: Crowds line the streets around St Paul's on Sunday 13th May as the King and Queen leave the Cathedral after a service of thanksgiving for the peace in Europe and prayers for a swift final end to the war. Europe was won and Germany defeated but Japan fought on in the Far East. Although threequarters of a million men were to be demobbed from the British Forces that year, many Britons were involved, with other Allied troops, especially Americans and Australians, in fighting the Japanese.

Left: On that Sunday churches were full. Overflow services were held outside many churches. Here people pray outside St Martin-in-the-Fields.

A FINAL END
TO THE WAR

Above: The Aldwych on
11th August 1945, 'snowed up'
by a rain of paper thrown
from offices along its length
following news of the defeat
of Japan. On 6th August an
atomic bomb had been
dropped on Hiroshima and
a second on Nagasaki on
9th August. All that was
awaited was the official
surrender by Japan.

Left: Following VE day the
war continued for a further
three months until Japan
surrendered on 14th August
1945. The war had lasted
just 20 days short of six years.
Once more there were
unrestrained celebrations.
This is the scene in Piccadilly
Circus at three o'clock in the
morning at the height of the
VJ Day celebrations.

DRESS REHEARSAL FOR CIVVY STREET

In April 1945 Western Command chiefs were given a demonstration of the demobilisation plans to enable men to be processed within 10 minutes. With millions of men to be returned to 'civvy street' it was important that the process be as swift and efficient as possible to avoid a backlog.

Opposite page top: A soldier signs in as the first step in his demobilisation.

Opposite page bottom: He is issued with pay, ration books, identity cards and health card.

Left: Being measured for a demob suit. Many men had been in service for the duration and had not had new civilian clothing for years.

Below: Being fitted with his choice of suit. The forces had to have produced millions of off-the-peg suits for demobbed men, consequently the fit and style were rarely perfect.

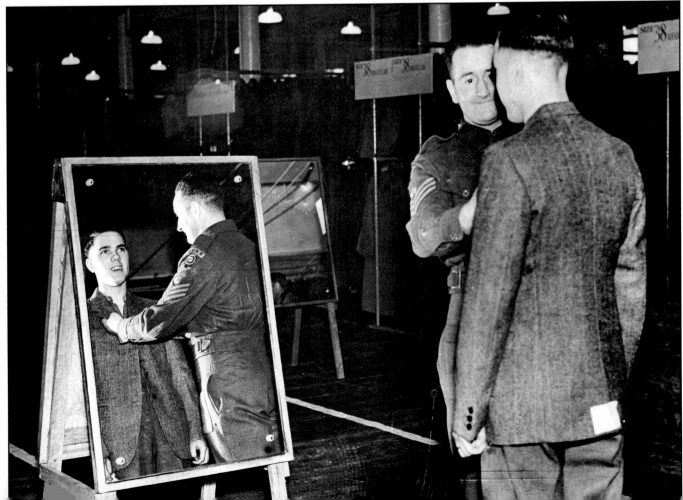

DEMOB HAPPY

Opposite page: Private H. Salter, being measured here is the first man to claim a 'non-austerity discharge suit'. Austerity Regulations had come into effect in March 1942 and dictated clothing styles which used a minimal amount of materials. Double-breasted styles, turn-ups on trousers and buttons simply for decoration were not permitted. However, by the time Private Salter was ready for discharge in October 1944, the war was going well enough for the regulations to be relaxed.

Left: And here is a happy Private Salter with his demob outfit.

Top: A 'Civvy Clothing Shop' was held at Olympia for demobbed soldiers to refashion their wardrobe. Here a soldier tries on a civilian suit jacket.

Above: Here he receives advice on that most important fashion accessory of the period - a hat. Advice was available from civilian personnel to ensure that the soldier returning to 'civvy street' would look the part.

EPILOGUE - MEMORIES

Opposite page top: 'Battle signatures' at a reunion of pilots from Biggin Hill in September 1946 at the White Hart Hotel at Brasted in Kent, which served as the flyers' unofficial headquarters during the war.

Opposite page bottom: The underground War Cabinet Rooms under Storey's Gate from where Churchill broadcast many of his stirring war speeches and from which, during the Blitz in particular, he, the cabinet and the Chiefs of Staff conducted the war. During the war its existence was kept secret, its location not revealed to the public until afterwards.

Above: The Operations Room, the pins on the map on the wall mark the position of ships and men when the war ended. On 16th August 1945 the lights were switched off for the first time since the shelter had come into commission in mid-1940 and the door was locked. In 1948 Parliament announced that the site was to be preserved. Up until 1981 access was restricted and many people had not even heard of it, but the complex has now been preserved and restored, and open is to the public to give people a flavour of what life was like for those in charge of the conduct of the war.

Left: Churchill's desk in Storey's Gate. The underground shelter covered six acres, housing 200 rooms, 40 feet below ground and protected by 17-ft thick reinforced concrete.

Bibliography

The People's War by Angus Calder, pub: Panther

How We Lived Then by Norman Longmate, pub: Hutchinson

Living Through the Blitz by Tom Harrisson, pub: Penguin

Children of the Blitz by Robert Westall, pub: Macmillan

The Blitz Then and Now (2 Volumes) ed. Winston Ramsay,
pub: After The Battle Publications

Blitz on Britain 1939-1945 by Alfred Price,
pub: Sutton Publications

Bombers and Mash by Raynes Minn, pub: Virago

War Papers introduced by Ludovic Kennedy, pub: Collins

Life on the Home Front by Tim Healey, pub: Readers Digest

Chronicle of the Twentieth Century edited by Derrick Mercer
pub: Longman